AF579752

The Bank Director

The Bank Director

Edited by
RICHARD B. JOHNSON

SMU PRESS • DALLAS

This is the second of a series on financial matters sponsored by the Foundation of the Southwestern Graduate School of Banking.

Library of Congress Cataloging in Publication Data
Main entry under title:

The Bank Director.

Papers presented at an assembly for bank directors or at a session of the Southwestern Graduate School of Banking.
Includes bibliographical references.

1. Bank management–Addresses, essays, lectures.
2. Business ethics–Addresses, essays, lectures.
3. Banks and banking–Addresses, essays, lectures.

I. Johnson, Richard Buhmann, 1913- ed.
II. Southwestern Graduate School of Banking.

HG1615.B33 658'.91'3321 74-14738
ISBN: 0-87074-145-4

Contents

Preface

ALL OF THE PRESENTATIONS in this book were first made to an Assembly for Bank Directors or a session of the Southwestern Graduate School of Banking. We have selected from among many excellent talks those which currently are most relevant to the bank director.

The talks are grouped in four sections: Codes and Responsibilities; Management Policies and Procedures; Credit Administration; and Trust Operations.

The Assemblies for Bank Directors are sponsored and supported by the Foundation of the Southwestern Graduate School of Banking. The first Assembly was held in Hot Springs, Arkansas, in November, 1968. Twenty Assemblies were held from 1969 to 1974, and three are scheduled for each year in the period from 1975 through 1981. The schedule for Assemblies in 1975 and 1976 is:

El Conquistador Hotel, San Juan, Puerto Rico, January 30–February 3, 1975.

The Homestead, Hot Springs, Virginia, May 25–29, 1975.

The Arizona Biltmore, Phoenix, Arizona, November 5–8, 1975.

The Sheraton-Waikiki and Royal Hawaiian, Honolulu, Hawaii, February 1–6, 1976.

The Broadmoor, Colorado Springs, Colorado, September 4–7, 1976.

The Breakers, Palm Beach, Florida, November 28–December 2, 1976.

The purpose of the Assembly for Bank Directors is: to increase the director's understanding of how he can serve his bank, to indicate the ways in which the director can best serve as a representative of his bank in the community, to provide better understanding of and respect for bank management's functions, and to acquaint the director fully with issues of critical interest to his bank and banking.

The Assemblies have been endorsed by the American Bankers Association, the Independent Bankers Association of America, and regional and state bankers associations.

RICHARD B. JOHNSON

Southwestern Graduate School of Banking
Southern Methodist University
October, 1974

PART ONE

Codes and Responsibilities

THEODORE BROWN

The Director and the Banking System

AN APPRAISAL of the role of the bank director should cover several different areas of responsibility. These can be grouped generally into three categories: the special characteristics of directorships in commercial banks, the bank director's responsibilities toward the community, and the director's role in relation to the officers and staff of the bank he represents.

Too frequently in history a bank directorship has been bestowed and accepted as something of a token of honor tendered a man who has achieved an enviable standard of financial and social status in the community. Although the appointment was in all likelihood not actually labeled as honorary, in many cases this was the prevailing attitude. Probably there was never a time in our financial history when that attitude was completely justifiable. However that may be, it is certain that in the complicated and trying times in which bankers live today there can be no justification for such an appointment or attitude.

In today's world, commercial banks are fighting hard to maintain their historic role as leaders of the financial community. They are faced with increasing pressures from competitive institutions which are eager to offer services that have heretofore been restricted to banks; pressures from state and federal legislators and members of regulatory agencies, some of whom would impose further restrictions in the name of the public interest; and even pressures from such sources as the President's Commission on Financial Institutions.

A bank director, particularly a nonmanagement director, has a greater opportunity and a greater responsibility today than at any period in recent history to help his or her institution in the struggle to maintain leadership. The wisdom, judgment, and experience at the command of our directors are potent tools and should be fully utilized if commercial banking is to retain its position of eminence in American finance.

To understand fully the scope of his opportunities and responsibilities, it is necessary that the director reflect for a moment upon the unique characteristics of a commercial bank as compared with the usual type of business corporation.

It is so fundamental that it is often overlooked that a bank's basic stock in trade consists of funds that are borrowed from others—its depositors. Because of this special characteristic, the federal government from its beginning, and each state as it formulated its statutes and regulations, imposed special rules upon the conduct of the banking business. Commercial banking always has been and probably always will be a highly regulated industry. The imposition of reasonable regulation in the public interest is not wrong and is not opposed by most bankers, but it does establish a climate for operations which may be foreign or uncomfortable to the director oriented toward private business or the professions. Therefore, one big demand upon the bank director is that he learn to recognize not only the legal restrictions, but the other implications that such regulation has upon his function and his bank's performance.

Bank management and bank directorship are so influenced by law and regulation that the very philosophy and approach to bank problems become colored by a consciousness of such regulation—probably short of a real concern about going to jail for violation of one of the many bank statutes, but certainly more acute than in most nonbank directorships.

Having to serve a variety of masters in filling his role does not make the bank director's job easier. As with any corporate directorship, he must act to protect the investment of the stockholders who elected him, and he has responsibilities to the bank staff to see that they are given adequate facilities and equipment to carry out their functions.

But above and beyond the usual corporate responsibilities, he has a responsibility to the bank's depositors and to the public to see that his bank is operated in such fashion that deposited funds are safeguarded and that public confidence in the American banking system is not put in peril.

The bank director, therefore, occupies a position quite different from that of a member of a trade association or public board, or even a typical corporate director. He may be an expert in finance, in a particular type of business, in education, in the professions or civil government, but his special expertise is not a license to represent any single interest in the conduct of his bank's affairs.

Rather, he is charged with the responsibility of representing all shareholders, majority and minority, and safeguarding all depositors, large and small.

Now, what are the different categories of bank directors, and how, if at all, do their functions differ?

Most banks in the United States include on their boards some so-called inside or management directors. Typically these are chosen from the senior executive officers of the bank, and usually they constitute a minority of the board members. Their special contribution to the deliberations of the board consists of an intimate knowledge of the daily operations of the bank and its current needs and problems. Their special responsibility is to see that the full board receives all the information, stated in current and accurate terms, that is necessary to conduct board business. Their special problem is that of wearing two hats successfully; that is, having the capacity to cope on the executive level with administrative problems, but also keeping the overriding policy objectives of the institution always in mind. This double-agent type of role requires a broad, adaptive, flexible mind and personality, because not infrequently overall policy may not jibe with the operating officer's notion of how things should be done on a day-to-day basis. For example, a board decision affecting compensation or hours to be worked may make great sense in the overall pattern but be hard for individuals to accept. The greatest contribution the officer-director can make to his bank is to serve as the bond joining together the two points of view.

The larger and probably more important classification of directors is the so-called outside director—the nonofficer director. These are the people who, in my judgment, assume the greater burden of responsibility, and are the people to whom we are really looking today for the greatest help and guidance. Aside from legal liabilities, their responsibility for guiding the major financial institutions of their respective communities is awesome.

In a typical situation, the outside director is expected to come in once a month and quickly review a mass of reports spanning thirty days or more of earnings, investments, loans, and special problems.

He is expected to spot weaknesses if any, make suggestions based upon his general business or community knowledge without interfering with the prerogative of management to run the daily show, and then leave the meeting with his confidential reports remaining on the table and his lips sealed. It is no small assignment, and one wonders occasionally why any outsider assumes the burden.

The special contribution of the outside director is, of course, his general knowledge of business, people, and community objectives in the trade area served by his bank. He can bring to management, which normally is pretty well confined to the bank premises during the business day, many valuable suggestions based upon his knowledge.

His special responsibility is to be alert and informed and to be a good questioner. A rubber-stamp director, though ever so prestigious in the community, is not really an effective director. The needler who asks pertinent questions when he doesn't understand management proposals or results, who questions management judgments in light of general business conditions, and who in effect keeps management on its toes is the ideal. To exercise the questioning technique without becoming an obstructionist and a bore to all the other directors requires good judgment, finesse, and timing.

We have already mentioned the fact that traditionally the bank director, by law and practice, has been charged with the responsibility of representing the interests of all shareholders and customers. This is not to say that boards should not contain a balance of experience, age, business, and social background. In banks and communities of all sizes, it is important for purposes of continuity and breadth of expression and representation that boards not be composed entirely of members of the same age group or social or business clique.

In very small banks with small boards it is frequently difficult to achieve a balance of all the desirable factors. In large banks with large boards it may be numerically easier, but just as difficult for other reasons, to achieve a theoretical balance. Nonetheless, a wide representation of age, experience, and business points of view provides strength for those institutions intent upon growth and dominance in their trade areas.

An interesting new development has begun to take place, however, with the recent emphasis on the proposal that bank boards be purposely structured to include representatives of specific groups. In some cases, the argument has been extended to promote the election of women directors as representatives of a special customer group. In other cases, demands have been made for the election of representatives of specific racial, religious, or age groups. Many banks do, of course, include women and persons of varying ethnic backgrounds on their boards, not because they are women or men or black or brown, but because they are otherwise qualified to assume the responsibilities of a bank director. Whether or not a director should be elected only because of sex or ethnic origin or religion is another question, one which should be carefully thought out in relation to the total responsibilities borne by bank directors.

Presentation of differing viewpoints provided by varying sex, ethnic, religious, and age backgrounds may be germane and helpful to the conduct of the bank's business, or it may be entirely irrelevant, obstructive, and simply lip service to contemporary and changing social mores. The business of the bank is the principal concern of the board of directors, and again it should be noted that the responsibilities of that business differ from the conduct of nonfinancial, nonquasi-public and nonregulated corporations.

It is often difficult to draw clear lines delineating the different areas of the director's responsibility. He certainly has responsibilities relating to the community as well as those relating to internal operations, but there is considerable overlap.

The typical example given has to do with the role the director should play in new business development. Certainly the most useful bank director is the one who is in a position to guide profitable new business to his bank. Guiding new business can take one of two forms: either the director serves as a conduit for information to be relayed to bank officers for action, or the director actually makes contact calls. The latter course may be the more unusual, but probably it is also the more impressive. It is not unusual and it can be very helpful for the director to accompany the officer on new business development calls instigated by the director.

To the extent that the director is successful in developing profitable new business, he is contributing to the growth of the bank; conversely, to the extent that the bank can serve the community through director contacts, it is enhancing the growth of the community and, incidentally, the director's reputation.

This brings up a question which is currently the subject of discussion in many board rooms: what are the proper limits of community involvement by commercial banks? Involvement can be manifested in many ways. To a great extent commercial banks have always been "involved" even before the word took on the semantic aura it now carries. Probably, though, more attention is now being given to the longer-term aspects of our involvement. Directors of rural banks and urban banks alike are being called upon to assume the role of statesmen in considering policies directed at improvement of economic and social conditions in their respective trade areas. In many instances it is difficult to show the results of such policies in current earnings statements, and this is the point at which the director's judgment becomes important. What should be his bank's position on a question which pits current earnings against less tangible long-term considerations? Student loans, minority business loans, low-cost housing loans, urban and rural development projects all present substantial problems of this nature for bank directors.

It could well be said that today's bank director must assume, more than ever before, some responsibility to the community at large to see that his bank functions as a positive contributory element of the community life. In addition to those local economic conditions that immediately affect bank growth and earnings, we are all affected by overriding problems such as educational opportunities, population density, pollution, drug abuse, etc., and we face a new responsibility for community leadership in such matters, even though they have never before been considered pertinent to banking.

Aside from the broad view of the bank director's role in modern banking, there are more specific aspects of his job as it relates to the bank itself.

First, because this point does overlap the effect upon the community as well as the effect on bank morale, there is the strict requirement of confidentiality placed upon the bank director. When a man or woman consents to serve as a bank director, he or she is placed in a position to share financial confidences that go to the heart of many a business and family in the community. At this point, the bank director assumes a professional responsibility akin to that of a legal advisor. Confidences exposed in the boardroom must remain there. Any temptation to spice up a luncheon or cocktail conversation with some relevant tidbits must be overcome. Casual gossip in the elevator, the locker room, or another business meeting simply cannot include items from the bank boardroom. For a bank director to perform otherwise is to do a disservice to his institution, to its customers, to the community, and to the tradition of American banking.

A question often arises regarding the optimum investment expected of a director in the stock of his bank. Probably there is no generally applicable answer. There are directors of banks who do not have anything more than qualifying shares yet who are excellent directors. In those cases, the investment is measured in terms of interest and integrity more than in dollars. Recently a successful professional corporate director was quoted as saying he would not accept a board seat in any company in which he did not feel he could safely invest $25,000. Such an arbitrary figure may not be possible in many small bank situations and may not be practical in larger banks. Although it is hard to equate dollars invested with performance achieved, it does seem that, to the extent possible, a good bank director should demonstrate confidence in his institution with an investment that is reasonable in his and its circumstances.

Heard and read so many times that it must seem tiresome is the statement that a bank director's principal function is to determine general policy. He does this by attending board meetings regularly and concentrating on the agenda prepared for the meeting. Not only does the consistently absent director expose himself to regulatory criticism and possible removal, but he negates by his absence the very purpose of his election. If, on the other hand, he attends in body but allows his mind to wander from the business at hand, he assumes the consequences of converting a business meeting into a gossip session.

The director who is serious about fulfilling his role will do more than vote for the selection of a chief executive officer and staff; he will do more than approve salary schedules and loan commitments. He will assume some responsibility for contributing to the long-range planning of his bank. Again, his knowledge of the trade area, its people and its economics, should be invaluable to the managing officers in formulating plans for the bank's continued growth and prosperity. He can be of great assistance as an extension of the eyes, ears, and judgment of the officers in measuring reaction to facility locations, new services, marketing programs, and other bothersome decisions.

It has been said many times, of course, that the most effective director recognizes that magic line between policy formation and policy administration. Sometimes the line is not easily defined and requires special sensitivity on the part of the director, particularly in those cases involving a new bank, new or young officers, or a change of operating procedures in an area with which the director is particularly expert. To be helpful in such cases without interfering with management authority requires great finesse, but it is also one of the greatest contributions a director can make.

Special sensitivity or intuition is also required of the director in determining how far he can go in the pursuit of his own business without taking unfair advantage of knowledge obtained by him as a director. To use information from credit files, trust department records, or other bank sources to get an advantage in dealing with the bank or its customers is to invite criticism if not legal action based on conflict of interest. Any sale of goods or services to the bank or its customers which even slightly resembles pressure bestowed by the cloak of authority of a directorship is poor taste and poor judgment, and generally can result only in unhappiness for the bank and the director. Any sale of goods or services to the bank itself, made by or on behalf of a director, must be at arm's length and must stand the scrutiny of the most inquisitive shareholder.

Also when conducting his personal banking business, the well-advised director seeks no special advantage from the bank officer. Interest rates, loan terms, service charges, etc., should be based upon the bank's standard policies and not upon special considerations requested by a director. In years past, it was not terribly unusual in many banks to give directors preferential treatment. To a considerable extent, this is disappearing largely because of disclosure requirements of bank supervisory and other government agencies. But where special considerations do exist, they should at least be extended uniformly under a policy that is open, aboveboard, known to all, and not the result of individual deals with individual directors.

A bank directorship should not be used to enhance an individual's reputation or to bolster his financial position. The acceptance of the position should include a willingness to relinquish it voluntarily in the event the individual's situation threatens the bank's reputation or becomes an embarrassment to other directors or bank officers. This includes a responsibility to recognize age and health as factors, to recognize changed personal or business finances as a factor, and to recognize present and potential conflicts of interest as a factor.

The responsibilities are awesome; in most instances the remuneration is not compensatory for those responsibilities; but the opportunity to be of real service to the bank, the banking system, and the community is impressive. Commercial banking, as we have known it in our nation's history, could not have played the role it has played in national development without the participation and contribution of able, dedicated bank directors.

Our immediate financial situation and probably the future era contain many difficult decisions for commercial banks, and the extent to which commercial banks continue to play a dominant role in the nation will depend greatly upon the quality of service rendered by the corps of directors of our banks.

HOMER J. LIVINGSTON

Moral Responsibilities in Banking

THE SUBJECT of the moral responsibilities in banking is one in which I have long had a personal and professional interest. In my judgment, the need for moral responsibility is more critical in banking than it is in most other businesses, since the possibilities for a conflict of interest are more frequently present. This subject is at the very heart of our business. This is particularly so for those in top management, since there is a strong tendency for those in an organization to accept the values of their superiors. "The crucial matter," as one observer put it, "is whether or not each individual comprising top management has a well-defined, high standard, personal code of behavior."[1] Banking is an exciting business, but it is also one of severe individual discipline.

We are living in a period of vast social change. Many of the old copybook maxims have been forgotten. We have revolted against rules. Someone has said that we are apostles of the experimental life. Certainly, the changes in banking in this generation have been almost unbelievable. Term loans, consumer credit, corporate and individual savings certificates of deposit, and direct lease financing are only a few of the new developments. With all the uncertainties and unsettlements of modern banking practice, we need to be certain that there is no disintegration in the underlying principles that govern the integrity and moral responsibility of the banker.

It is nothing short of willful self-delusion to assume that the public is not deeply aware of the constant need for the highest sense of moral responsibility in banking. The banker collects the individual and corporate savings of the American people and determines how they will flow safely and productively into the economic life of the nation.

It might be useful, at the outset, to review a definition or two. *Moral*, according to Webster, relates to making the distinction between right and wrong in conduct, while *responsibility* implies being accountable to someone. The commercial banker occupies a unique position in our society and this, in large measure, determines his accountability. For example, a banker is accountable to his stockholders, as is any corporate officer. But in addition, as an official of a quasi-public financial institution he is also accountable for the safety of the depositor's funds, and this imposes limitations on his management prerogatives. The people who entrust their life savings to the banker have an understandable concern for their safety. The near-fiduciary quality that characterizes most of the banker's official as well as community relationships imposes rigorous and rigid moral standards on his conduct.

The banker in his official capacity is guardian, so to speak, of the savings of the community, as both corporate and personal funds are entrusted to him for safekeeping. As the lender of funds, the banker is the confidant of businessmen and other borrowers in the community. There are numerous possibilities for a conflict of interest to arise in just this one area.

As the principal financial officer in the community, the banker becomes a financial adviser to government at all levels. As a trust officer, he has grave responsibilities both to the donor and to the beneficiary. Not only is he to manage funds as directed, but he also has the obligation to invest the principal to insure both safety and income. In discharging this responsibility, he has the opportunity to channel funds into a broad spectrum of investments. In selecting investments—in choosing one as against another—the possibility of a conflict of interest is great. Why should the banker not select for investment the shares of a company or enterprise that is close to the bank as against one that is not? What, other than personal integrity, is to prevent the investment officer from recommending the securities of a company in which the banker and his family have a financial interest?

In his unofficial activities in the community, too, the commercial banker is confronted with decisions which require a keen sense of personal and moral responsibility. He is adviser and consultant to a seemingly ever growing circle of organizations—business, welfare, civic, community, educational, and cultural. Moreover, friends and acquaintances seek the banker's judgment, based on the experience flowing from his position in the community. He is asked to serve as director or trustee of business corporations, united appeal funds, school boards, churches, hospitals, universities, and art museums, all having balances and investments in which his bank, and he personally, may have a financial interest.

Consider the specific instance where the chief executive officer of a bank is a member of the board of directors of a major company in the community. Not only may this firm be an important customer, but the chief executive officer of the company also may be a member of the board of directors of the bank. The possibility of a conflict of interest in these circumstances is great.

And then there are those peculiar personal relationships where the banker becomes adviser and consultant to widows, orphans, and others—persons who at times attribute to the banker qualities approaching omniscience.

This brief review of the types of problems confronting the banker indicates the countless opportunities for the development of conflicts of interest in his day-to-day activities. It also makes apparent the impossibility of specifically enumerating all of them. On the other hand, it is possible to outline the moral principles that should govern and characterize the conduct of a banker.

In a very broad sense, this task of codifying laws to govern behavior is a subject that men have pondered and struggled with over the ages. Basically, however, the answer lies in our Judaeo-Christian heritage, which is an essential part of our culture. It is upon this that personal integrity rests, and this, in turn, is the foundation of more specific codes that may be defined. Such codes, I might add, can only be looked upon as minimal standards. In the last analysis, no written code can take the place of personal integrity.

A few years ago, my associates and I at the First National Bank of Chicago attempted to set down in writing some basic principles which are essential to the highest personal conduct. We prepared this memorandum for distribution to our staff. It was an effort to insure a continuation of the reputation of the bank by restating long-standing policies. In doing so, it was our intention to alert all personnel to possible conflicts of interest.

In the area of investments and customer relationships, a banker (or the members of his immediate family) should not invest in the securities of any customer where such an investment could even remotely influence his business judgment in dealing with that customer. For instance, except in the case of securities registered on a national exchange and with a broad market, it obviously would be improper for a lending officer to invest in the securities of a corporation that the bank is financing. Moreover, even if the relationship between a particular bank officer and the customer is such that the possibility of influencing a transaction is remote, public disclosure of the investment might be adversely interpreted.

In the last few years there has been quite a surge of so-called acquisitions by one corporation of another, for purposes of diversification or for other reasons. A developing technique in this area has been the secret acquisition by the acquiring corporation of shares of the company which it seeks, usually through purchases on the stock exchanges. When the acquiring corporation has thus been able to obtain a substantial block of stock of the company it seeks, it then makes a public offer to the shareholders of the company at a price high enough above the traded market value of that company's shares to make the acceptance of the offer attractive to its shareholders. Since, in many instances, the amount of money required by the acquiring corporation is very substantial, it is often necessary for the corporation to arrange with its bankers to borrow the money for this purpose. Thus, the banker knows his customer intends to offer a price substantially higher than the market value and that the corporation will be able to finance the purchase of such shares as may be tendered to it because the banker has arranged the necessary financing. In these circumstances, the banker's temptation personally to buy shares of stock of the company to be thus acquired is great indeed, since there is virtually a guaranteed profit between the current market value of such shares and the amount the acquiring corporation proposes to offer.

There is certainly a moral if not a legal duty on the part of the banker not to take advantage of his knowledge of the proposed transaction for his personal benefit. The New York Stock Exchange has presented the following guidelines in its booklet, *The Corporate Director and the Investing Public*:

> Where a development of major importance is expected to reach the appropriate time for announcement within the next few months, transactions by officers and directors should be avoided.
>
> . . . The considerations that affect officer and director transactions in stock of their own company may be pertinent to transactions in the shares of other companies with whom discussions of acquisition, merger or important contracts, etc., are being considered or carried on.

While the stock exchange booklet is primarily addressed to transactions by officers and directors of the involved company, the principle applies with no less force as a guide to the conduct of the banker in the circumstances I have described. Mr. Mark Garlinghouse, Vice-President and General Counsel of Southwestern Bell, made a highly relevant observation five years ago. He noted, "In the long run, it is not enough that the businessman view his own activities as moral and legal. What is important is that the public also view those activities as moral and legal."[2]

The National Bank Act provides that it is a criminal offense for any officer, director, or employee of a bank to accept "any fee, commission, gift or thing of value" for procuring, or endeavoring to procure, any loan or extension of credit.

Some of us receive gifts at Christmas or at other times from some of our customers, including borrowers and others who are furnishing supplies, equipment, or services to the bank. Many banks and corporations strictly prohibit the acceptance of any gifts whatsoever. Whatever policy you follow, it is important that you and all your associates understand its limitations. In our own institution, no officer or employee may accept loans, services, excess entertainment or travel, or gifts of substantial value from any individual or company doing business with the bank. Although some embarrassment is occasionally involved, gifts other than those of small value are required to be returned to the customer with an appropriate explanation of bank policy. The determination of whether the value of the gift is such that it can be retained or whether it should be returned to the donor is left to the good judgment of the individual involved.

There are obvious possibilities for conflicts of interest developing where a banker becomes associated with another corporation or business enterprise as an officer or director. The bylaws of our bank prohibit any officer or employee from serving as a director or employee of any other business organization (other than those affiliated with the bank) unless he has the prior consent of the bank's executive committee. One of the principal reasons for the existence of this bylaw is the fact that when an officer or employee of the bank is affiliated with an outside company, it may give the impression that the bank is financially interested in the enterprise, or is financially supporting it. At the very least, such service by the bank officer tends to put the imprimatur of the bank on the strength of the company and the integrity of its management. In general, the bank does not approve of its officers and employees being in any way associated with outside commercial enterprises. As a result, approvals are granted only in special circumstances.

The manifold and diverse activities of the trust department, where a fiduciary relationship characterizes most operations, give rise to countless conflict of interest problems. One of my associates is currently preparing a study on conflict of interest problems in only one area, namely, between the trust department and the commercial department of the bank itself. Just an outline of this subject with the legal citations covers six pages. Moreover, he tells me that there are well over a thousand cases on only one point, the duty of the trustee to give undivided loyalty to his trust. As you know, this is generally regarded as the most important principle in the law of trusts.

The varying problems presented by this fundamental duty of loyalty have been with us for a long time.[3] Here again, one can go back to one of the earliest reported cases of such loyalty, which is found in the sixteenth chapter of the Gospel according to Saint Luke. In the King James version, it reads as follows:

> There was a certain rich man, which had a steward; and the same was accused unto him that he had wasted his goods.
>
> And he called him, and said unto him, How is it that I hear this of thee? give an account of thy stewardship; for thou mayest be no longer steward.

Since that time, the cases on divided loyalty and self-dealing have been legion. In fact, the case law on conflict of interest makes up a major part of the law on administration of estates and trusts.[4]

We believe that if a bank customer executes a will or trust agreement designating the bank as executor or trustee, and names as beneficiary (or legatee or devisee) any bank officer or employee (or member of his immediate family) who is unrelated by blood or marriage, the employee must renounce his interest in the will or agreement.

Any officer or employee of the bank who is named as executor or as trustee by any customer of the bank, not related to the officer or employee by blood or marriage, may not accept such appointment without the prior approval of one of the executive officers of the trust department.

One of the fastest growing areas in banking today involves pension and profit sharing trust funds. Compounding the difficulty of making wise investment decisions is the question of whether or not the fund should be invested in the donor company's own stock. An even more difficult question involves the purchase of the company's own stock before a contemplated acquisition by the company of another firm. A decision to buy the company's own stock might drive up the price before negotiations for the acquisition are to begin. Since the acquisition is to be accomplished by an exchange of stock, it is obvious how this action could benefit the company seeking to acquire another company.

There is likewise the question of the purchase by a corporate trustee of its own stock as a trust investment and the retention of such stock previously purchased by the settlor. The purchase of such stock by the trustee has almost universally been held a violation of the duty of loyalty, while retention has frequently been sustained on the basis of state statute or authorization from the settlor. Where the trust instrument contains language specifically authorizing the trustee to retain its own share in the trust estate, virtually all of the cases and commentators agree that the trustee is protected.[5]

The absence of definitive case law to guide a corporate trustee and the differing attitudes and approaches of the leading academic authorities on trust law present the corporate trustee with many difficult conflict of interest questions.

Finally, I should like to comment briefly on the "cease and desist legislation" that has recently been introduced in the Congress. This bill provides for the use of cease and desist orders for the suspension and removal of bank officers and directors, and the preclusion of a person's participation in the conduct of a bank's affairs. It reflects, unfortunately, the fact that the banking industry has recently attracted "an increased number of ill-purposed individuals whose aims are contrary to the best interests of the banks and the public."[6] The proposal is the response of the regulatory agencies to situations where persuasion by the supervisory authorities has been insufficient to birng about cessation or correction of unsound or imprudent practices. In principle, I am sympathetic with the objectives of this proposed legislation.

Recent incidents, such as the much publicized failure of the San Francisco National Bank, dramatically illustrate the consequences of the absence of personal integrity and the sordid aftermath of irresponsibility. The proposed Financial Institutions Supervisory Act of 1966—the cease and desist bill—is a direct response to this breakdown of moral responsibility in the management of particular banks. The San Francisco National Bank's failure resulted in potential monetary losses to innocent depositors. Equally serious, however, it tarnished the reputation of banks and bankers in general. It has strengthened the argument of those who wish to regulate the industry even more closely. It is imperative, therefore, that we as bankers and members of senior management individually strive to observe an even more exacting code of ethics. Moreover, we must demand observance of such a code by our associates. This is a responsibility we cannot avoid.

Occasionally, under the pressure of day-to-day operations—concern about accommodating borrowers during a period of tight money, the rising cost of funds, problems of successor management, loan deposit ratios, and the countless other problems that cross the banker's desk daily—there is a danger that inadequate attention may be given to possible conflicts of interest and to the banker's moral responsibility.

In a period of continued boom and prosperity, rigid principles of integrity and a high sense of responsibility may also seem a trifle old-fashioned. An entire nation may become exclusively absorbed in the goods and chattels of prosperity. The spirit of getting yours while the getting is good, of approaching the margin of what is right, of cutting sharp corners, may seem irresistible. With our amazing progress, it is easy to become so complacent and so self-satisfied that we may not be aware of a steady erosion of our moral responsibility as bankers.

There is the subtle temptation of big deposit totals, bidding for short-term deposits at the highest permissible interest rates and then seeking longer term, less desirable, and less liquid assets to keep ahead of mounting interest costs. There is the temptation to purchase for a fast turnover a speculative "sure thing" as an investment. There is the temptation to accept a poor risk loan because of the pressure of important friends of the bank. There is the temptation to delay writing off at once a loan whose repayment is doubtful, and the temptation to do window dressing of public statements of the bank's condition.

The conduct of the banker as he confronts such problems must be clearly predictable. His community must feel confident of where he will stand as he faces the stresses and strains that are involved in major decisions affecting women and children with their estates, businesses whose success or failure depends on credit, and municipalities whose fiscal soundness may rest on the wisdom of his counsel. Only when his integrity is beyond question does he deserve and can he command the complete trust of his community.

From the establishment of this nation, American business has succeeded beyond its fondest dreams. Its record constitutes an inspiring illustration of how a people, given justice, liberty, and incentive, have enriched life and raised the whole level of their economic well-being. The great revolutionists of our time have been American businessmen whose enterprises are creating wealth for the masses and increasing leisure and freedom. No longer is it necessary in this nation for our people to devote their entire energies and most of their time to the primary task of providing themselves with food, clothing, and shelter. Our people have been emancipated by the products of industry from the hardest physical labor and drudgery.

The bankers of the nation have played a significant role in this development. They have supplied the capital that has enabled American industry to produce an endless flow of goods for the masses. They have helped to broaden consumption, elevate living standards, and increase the economic welfare of the American people beyond anything ever previously achieved. They have helped millions of Americans to a security and richness of life not approached by the masses in any other land or age. But they have played an even greater role in setting high standards for moral integrity and conscientious stewardship.

We must never underestimate those higher values which lie beyond the economics and statistics of banking. Integrity is a bank's most valuable asset. Only if we merit this reputation can we be certain that banking will maintain the confidence and trust of the American people and a position of distinguished leadership in the American economy.

This address was delivered at the Southwestern Graduate School of Banking, Dallas, Texas, July 18, 1966. At the time of his death, Homer J. Livingston was Chairman of the Board (retired) of the First National Bank in Chicago.

NOTES

1. Raymond C. Baumhart, "How Ethical Are Businessmen?" *Harvard Business Review* (July-August 1961): 6.
2. Mark Garlinghouse, "The Moral Issue in Business," Southwestern Graduate School of Banking (1961).
3. See Scott, *The Fiduciary Principle*, 37 Cal. L. Rev. 539 (1949).
4. Walter D. Fletcher, "Divided Loyalty and Self-Dealing," *Trusts and Estates* 54 (March 1955): 234.
5. See William W. Helms, "Retention of Own Stock in Trust," *Trusts and Estates* 51 (May 1962): 434.
6. U.S., Congress, Senate, Subcommittee of the Committee on Banking and Currency, Statement by J. L. Robertson: *Hearing on S. 3158*, 1966, p. 38.

MURRAY KYGER

Moral Responsibilities and Standards Of Ethics in Commercial Banking

THE SUBJECT of moral responsibilities and standards of ethics in commercial banking is not something which has just come into being during the last few years. It is simply a matter of our courts and public opinion focusing attention on the problem. Current developments demand that businessmen in general, and commercial bankers in particular, give the subject much closer attention. Those of us in banking need to stay abreast of all such developments, not just within the corporate banking structure but also outside of the field of commercial banking.

On November 18, 1971, under the auspices of the Conference Board, a session was held to deal with the broad subject, "The Board of Directors: New Challenges, New Directions." Outstanding executives considered many different facets of this subject. One speaker referred to several of the major corporate problems, including those of Penn Central and Lockheed, which had confronted our country within the preceding few months. This gentleman stated:

> In my judgment they [corporate problems] could have been averted or mitigated in the past, and they can be in the future, with greater board effectiveness in helping management weigh the big decisions. . . . On the really big decisions, they [the board] must bear down hard on management, to make sure that the risk/reward ratio is favorable and that the company's capacity to absorb a failure is adequate to insure survival. . . . The board's role in selecting the Chief Executive Officer and auditing his performance is a responsibility which the board cannot escape.

In the March-April 1972 issue of the *Harvard Business Review*, there are two excellent articles dealing with corporate responsibility. The first, entitled "The President and the Board of Directors," opens with this statement: "Boards of Directors have been part of our business scene for over 150 years, but their functions have not been clearly defined and generally accepted through practice in the management of corporations."

The author of the article, Professor Myles L. Mace, first describes briefly what he found boards to be actually doing and takes note of the disparity between theory and practice. He then discusses what directors fail to do in properly discharging their responsibilities. Of great importance is his identification of the critical and controlling role of the president of a corporation. He makes the point that even when a board of directors does not discharge all of its functions exactly as it should, there is no question that it has a disciplinary value, motivating the company managers to do a better job of thinking through their problems and of being prepared with solutions, explanations, or rationales. Professor Mace states that one president with whom he communicated described the disciplinary value of the outside board member in this way: "The fact that you know that outside directors are going to be looking at what you have done, and what you are doing, forces you to do a little better job." According to Professor Mace, some corporate executives refer to their board of directors as the "corporate conscience."

For those presidents and boards of directors who do want the directors to perform more than passive functions and to give meaning and implementation to the legal statement, "the board shall manage," Professor Mace offers this five-point program:

1. Ask all insiders on the Board other than the Chairman and the President to resign from the Board.
2. See to it that the specific functions of the Board are discussed and agreed upon by the Chairman, the President and the outside Board members, and reduced to writing as a charter to board activities.
3. Establish the criteria by which the Board is required to evaluate the performance of the President annually, on a formal basis.
4. Directors should ask those discerning questions of presidents at board meetings that they would ask if they owned a substantial part of the companies on which they serve as directors—that is, the questions owners would ask.
5. Establish compensation rates for outside directors which motivate them to fulfill active and responsible roles as directors.

In this same issue of the *Harvard Business Review*, Alonzo McDonald of McKinsey & Company has an article entitled "Conflict at the Summit: A Deadly Game." In the foreword to this article is the comment: "Until management is motivated to accept a new code of ethics and conduct for those in the Executive Suite, the disease of destructive conflict at the top cannot be cured." Mr. McDonald makes this somewhat startling statement: "The fact is that top management does not want to be organized; and when it is organized in any company, it does not stay that way for long."

In 1965, *Newsweek* magazine, in cooperation with the National Industrial Conference Board, now referred to as the Conference Board, set out to find the answer to an important question: "What do Americans really think of business?" This study was introduced with the statement, "A storm is brewing in the minds of millions of Americans. It is small now—a cloud no bigger than a vague dissatisfaction. But it may swirl up angrily on the horizon for American business management." As we reflect on this statement, it is not difficult to conclude that here we have a prophecy of disturbing business developments in banking and industry which have received and are receiving national publicity and congressional investigation.

In behalf of *Newsweek* and the Conference Board, the well-known opinion analysis firm of Louis Harris & Associates surveyed two thousand people in an attempt to answer the question: "What do Americans really think of business?" This survey produced some reactions which are definitely relevant to moral responsibilities in commercial banking. Serious consideration should be given to a few excerpts from these opinions, such as: "Business is respected, but not always trusted," and "42% of those interviewed agree that most businessmen will do anything, honest or not, for a buck." And in response to the question, "Has business helped raise moral standards?" the answers were anything but complimentary. Sixty-two percent of those interviewed were reported as having the feeling that business needs to "raise moral standards."

During the last few months, headlines in the *American Banker*, leading articles in the *Wall Street Journal*, and a great deal of additional publicity have told us that today we do have problems relating to moral responsibilities in corporate life. This is especially true where commercial bankers are concerned. We have seen dramatized such terms as "equity kickers," "piece of the action," "self-dealing," "disclosure," "insider information," and "interlocking directors."

The corporate entity is very important to our American economic development and progress. Broadly speaking, business enterprise involves proprietorships, partnerships, and corporations. I would be the first to say that the proprietorship and partnership play a most important role in our business scene, and small businesses should be encouraged and protected against unfair competition. However, mass production and the ability to meet international competition emphasize the importance of large capital and its resulting resources. Capital ownership through stockholders results in a twofold accomplishment: first, through shareholders, we have a pooling of investment which has made possible our large commercial and industrial industries; secondly, the corporate vehicle has given the average American the opportunity to be an investor in such important operations as the American Telephone and Telegraph Company, General Motors, and many others.

The corporation is owned by its shareholders, who elect a board of directors. The board in turn is responsible for the affairs of the corporation, and in particular it is responsible for providing competent management. More and more, we are hearing of the "outside director" and his responsibility. Legally, the board of directors is responsible for corporate conduct, and yet the management selected by the board of directors is the nerve center of corporate activity and must assume the major role in seeing to it that the board of directors and particularly "outside directors" understand and are placed in a position to discharge their responsibility.

I mention corporate organizations solely for the purpose of placing on management the spotlight of responsibility in this matter of seeing to it that the board of directors (both collectively as a board and individually) thoroughly understands the responsibility of the board, and then, more importantly, helps the board to discharge this responsibility. In light of developments on this whole subject of moral responsibilities in corporate affairs, I take real pride in what we have been doing through the Assemblies for Bank Directors over a period of some five years.

In July, 1966, the late Homer J. Livingston, in his capacity as Chairman of the First National Bank of Chicago, honored our Southwest Graduate School of Banking by addressing the Evening Series Lectures on the subject, "Moral Responsibility in Banking." Mr. Livingston had this to say:

Banking is an exciting business, but it also is one of severe individual discipline.

The near fiduciary quality that characterizes most of the banker's official as well as community relationships imposes rigid moral standards on his conduct.

. . . no written code can take the place of personal integrity.

In 1970, the Robert Morris Associates issued a booklet on the question of conflicts of interest from the point of view of banks and bankers. The somewhat ominous title of this publication is *Danger—Pitfalls Ahead.* In the preface of this book, the following comment is made:

With increasing frequency these days, people are finding the propriety of their ethics, their official actions, and their personal finances questioned in public. . . . The Banking industry can and should police itself in this field. . . . One advisory service informs us that only one-third of the major financial institutions in the United States have written policy statements applicable to officer, employee and director situations with reference to conflict of interest and moral responsibilities.

At the October, 1970, meeting of the American Bankers Association in Miami, Florida, the retiring president of the association indicated that moral and ethical standards in corporate life have become so important that the association needed to provide guidance and leadership to its members on this particular subject. Just one year later, in the fall of 1971, the American Bankers Association issued a booklet entitled *The Drafting of a Banker's Code.* The following statements appeared in this publication:

A bank is judged by the collective and individual performance of its directors, officers, and employees. Thus, bankers traditionally have recognized that their first duty to the bank, its customers, and its shareholders is to act in all things in a manner that merits public trust and confidence.

Every bank has a code of conduct which is followed by its officers and employees, whether or not the code has been reduced to writing.

The clear purpose of the ABA booklet is to encourage banks to adopt a statement of policy on the important matter of ethical behavior and moral responsibilities.

In 1864, and this is certainly historical, the first Comptroller of the Currency of the United States, Hugh M'Culloch, addressed a communication to the banks making up the national banking system at that time. His communication was entitled "Suggestions to the Managers of Banks." These suggestions were not referred to as a code of ethics, but they definitely incorporated certain admonitions which were in this category. For example, these were some of his words of advice:

> Do nothing to foster and encourage speculation.
>
> Give facilities only to legitimate and prudent transactions.
>
> If you have reason to distrust the integrity of a customer, close his account. Never deal with a rascal under the impression that you can prevent him from cheating you. The risk in such cases is greater than the profits.
>
> In business, know no man's politics.

While none of us had the pleasure of knowing Mr. M'Culloch, I think we can all agree that he was capable of giving good advice. Many excellent follow-up points to these suggestions from the first Comptroller of the Currency can be found in the current publication of the Comptroller entitled "Duties and Liabilities of Directors of National Banks." The latest copy of this publication was revised in October, 1969, and whether you are a national or a state bank director, you would make no mistake in reviewing this publication.

The most valuable and helpful tool for direction and guidance that is available to those of us in commercial banking who seek to discharge our duties from the point of view of directors and management is the publication of the American Bankers Association entitled *A Bank Director's Job.* From April, 1956, through August, 1967, most of the chapters which make up the publication appeared as articles in *Banking,* the official monthly publication of the American Bankers Association. Herbert Bratter was the author of the articles, but in preparing them he had help from such sources as the Comptroller of the Currency, the Federal Deposit Insurance Corporation, and the Federal Reserve Board. The editor of *Banking* stated that the primary purpose of the articles, and later the booklet, was to: (1) help orient the new bank director; (2) give the experienced bank director a new angle on his job; and (3) assist top management by making directors aware of their responsibilities toward shareholders, depositors, management, and the general public.

In the first chapter of this booklet, dealing with "Legal Responsibilities," the statement is made that the common law imposes many responsibilities on bank directors, particularly because of the special nature and importance of banking. These comforting words are added:

"The director who exercises reasonable and ordinary care does not expose himself. . . ." But he should "scrupulously avoid self-serving practices."

In the chapter entitled "Care and Diligence," it is stated that the bank director should bring his "business experience to bear on the bank's affairs as common sense dictates." The bank director is referred to as a "Trustee of the interest of the shareholders."

In the chapter entitled "Over-all Policy," the opening paragraph states: "In a bank, the director's duty is to direct and not to lead. The officers are charged with carrying out the directors' policies. They must be ever alert to insure that the policies are being faithfully, ably, and honestly executed by bank personnel."

One of the most important chapters in this booklet, "Let Management Manage," offers some good advice: "While responsible for loan policy, they [the directors] are not expected to pass upon each and every loan made by the bank. . . . If those in management are capable, the directors should leave them alone in the details of operating the bank. . . . One thing is clear: the directors cannot manage the bank."

The following important observations are made in the chapter captioned "At the Bank Directors' Meeting:"

> The Board of Directors in a bank will function in a satisfactory manner if its members are made aware of their duties and realize that it is they who should establish policies for the bank and see that those policies are carried out by the officers. . . .
>
> The director should know what is going on in the bank and its environment.

There are some unusually fine pieces of advice in the chapter entitled "Lending Policy." One comment very pertinent to the subject we are discussing is this: "Loans to directors and officers need to be surrounded with circumspection. No other type of loan is scrutinized more carefully by bank examiners. The charging of a lower rate of interest on loans to directors and officers than on loans to others of equal credit worthiness is hard to justify."

In discussing general responsibilities of the directors, a most important chapter, captioned "Earnings, Expenses and Dividends," makes the old-fashioned statement that "their first consideration should be protection of depositors who supply more than 90% of the funds used in banking."

There is also an excellent chapter on "Personnel," which gives good advice to this effect: "Among other personnel questions in which directors should take an interest is the matter of outside business interests. A bank officer or employee should not also be in another business; nor should he engage in speculative ventures."

The whole discussion in "Insider Trading," a new chapter in this thirteenth edition of the booklet, is excellent with respect to moral responsibilities. One sentence stands out above all others: "Essentially, the matter boils down to using good judgment and common sense. The bank director, like the banker, should ask himself whether using certain inside information is the right or the wrong thing to do." Incidentally, we can apply this same test to almost any question which comes up in the field of moral and ethical standards.

Admittedly, we have been talking about some rather sobering points relative to moral responsibility and ethics in banking. What we should remember and emphasize to ourselves is that we make better representatives and spokesmen for the banking industry if we are aware of the fundamental responsibilities which are clearly enunciated and discussed in this booklet, *A Bank Director's Job.*

Where management enables the directors to be well informed and instrumental in setting policy, we have no problem. The key to the whole matter is an interested and informed board of directors and competent management.

JACK T. CONN

Integrity, the Cornerstone of Banking

BANK MANAGEMENT is divided on the fundamental issue of the appropriate consistency and functions of boards of directors. There are many chief executive officers who would apply the old clichés, "Ignorance is bliss" and "Silence is golden."

As for board members, they consider a little knowledge to be a dangerous thing and much knowledge akin to Dante's inferno. They would have as their directors those who keep large deposits in the bank and favor short and jolly board meetings at which no one questions the sagacity of management or the infallibility of its decisions. They would choose those who are warm in praise of the growth and viability of the bank and the participation of bank personnel in civic affairs. They would elect to their boards those in such high income tax brackets that a penurious dividend policy (perhaps dictated by low earnings) would not occasion criticism. Above all, they would avoid those who ask questions. Such managing officers would concur with Shakespeare's Caesar, who said:

> "Let me have men about me that are fat:
> Sleek-headed men and such as sleep o' nights:
> Yond Cassius has a lean and hungry look;
> He thinks too much: such men are dangerous."

We believe, on the other hand, that directors who are knowledgeable in the area of banking criteria, who are cognizant of the role banks should play in the development of their communities, and who are aware of their functions and responsibilities as bank directors make a substantial, valuable, and needful contribution to commercial banking.

What are your powers, your duties, your responsibilities? Since the primary obligation of every bank is to protect the funds of its depositors, your chief responsibility is to insure the soundness and integrity of the loans and investments of your bank. To carry out your responsibility and your prime obligation, you should be furnished with adequate information at your board meetings.

I cannot overemphasize the fact that the note case is the very foundation of every bank. If the bank has ever increasing losses, if its note case contains more and more questionable loans which are lacking in security and without clear sources of repayment, then the bank itself will begin to crumble. No bank has greater strength than its loans. When too much of its paper is classified, the bank cannot grow, it cannot build. Morale of personnel is sharply diminished—no one wants to be a part of a failing bank. When classified paper reaches an untenable amount, the board of directors will be called upon to increase the capital of the bank. It is most difficult to sell stock in a bank which is in trouble; therefore, the demand to increase capital is factually a stock assessment. Finally, if the bank fails, and the members of the board have not acted with reasonable prudence and diligence, they may be jointly and severally liable for losses to depositors and the FDIC.

In preserving the integrity of the note case, there is no single document more important to you as a bank director than the report of the bank examiner. If that report indicates that the total classified paper exceeds 25% of the bank's capital structure (capital, surplus, undivided profits, reserve for loan losses, and subordinated capital debentures), then immediate rectification is indicated. If it exceeds 50% you are in great trouble, and you may deem it necessary to consider a change in management or the appointment of an executive committee from the board to aid management. You must constantly be on the alert for increases in classified paper. Many good and well-managed banks may at times have too many classified loans. This in itself is not occasion for alarm. But a continuing deterioration in the loan portfolio is occasion for alarm and usually warrants a change in management and a change in loan policies.

In the 1940s there was a rule of thumb that a bank should hold one-third in cash, one-third in loans, and one-third in bonds. Economic forces have invalidated that rule. Today if your loans are relatively short-term and in the main are fully protected by marketable collateral, a loan to deposit ratio of 60% to 70% is not objectionable.

The Office of the Comptroller of the Currency has prepared a liquidity analysis formula which will be quite helpful to you in determining the liquidity posture of your bank. If you are a director of a national bank, you should receive a report of the bank's liquidity at each monthly meeting. If you are a director of a state bank, I would advise you to request your management to prepare such a report and present it. If the analysis reflects less than 20% liquidity, that is a warning which should not be disregarded.

To protect the bank against recessions sure to come with a resultant increase in charge-offs and losses, you should insist that your bank maintain a reserve for bad debts in a range equaling 1% to 2% of loans outstanding. Certainly, the bank should annually add to its reserves the full amount of tax-exempt income permitted under federal statute.

From what I have said you should not conclude that a commercial bank should operate without loan losses. Such a bank is no more than a depository. It does not fulfill its obligations to its community. The bank cannot grow, and neither can its community. While there are no hard and fast rules, charge-offs from 0.25% to 0.75% of installment loans and up to 0.5% of commercial and real estate loans are acceptable. In determining your bank's charge-offs under the criteria stated, you should take a five year average. You should also determine the percentage of recoveries of loans charged off. As a historical average, recoveries should be about 50% of charge-offs.

The integrity of a bank is also dependent upon its investments. To some degree liquidity in bond portfolios is measurable by maturities. If a composite of your government and municipal obligations reflects that less than 50% mature within five years, then the board should question the investment policy. At least every six months you should require a report reflecting the book value and the market value of the bank's bond portfolio, and at each meeting the board should be apprised of bonds purchased and sold during the preceding month. In banks of a size not warranting the full-time employment of an investment officer, management should be encouraged to rely upon the advice and counsel of its principal correspondent bank.

Commercial banking is a business affected by the public interest, and in some respects it is *sui generis*. Banking assets are attributable to the deposits of the members of the community served by the bank. The unique power to create deposits by making loans enables banks in effect to create money. More than 98% of all bank depositors are protected against loss by the Federal Deposit Insurance Corporation. Banks are protected against injurious competition by state and federal regulatory agencies. These unique powers and protective features have been granted upon the premise that banks will supply the credit requisite to the growth of their communities and the nation. Banking integrity commands faithful observance of this responsibility. As board members you are charged with the duty of insisting that your bank meet legitimate credit demands. You should be aware that banks which are not concerned with the growth of their communities are parasitical. They are in the position of living off the community without contributing to it.

Another element of banking integrity is the maintenance of adequate capital structure. While there are many tests of adequacy, a fairly safe rule is the measurement of capital against loans. If your capital, surplus, undivided profits, and reserve for loan losses equal 1/7th or a greater fraction of your total loans, and your note case and investment portfolio meet the criteria herein stated, then your capital structure is adequate. To maintain capital adequacy, you should give consideration to earnings and dividends. In banks of $50,000,000 or less in total assets, the net operating income should be an amount equalling 1% of total assets. The law of diminishing returns operates against larger banks. Under another standard your bank's net operating income should equal 10% to 12% of the capital, surplus, and undivided profits. It is never wise to pay dividends of more than 50% of net operating income. If your bank is experiencing dramatic growth, it is probable that retention of earnings will not meet capital requirements. The management and the board must then devise and implement other means of injecting additional capital.

The primary obligation of the board of directors is to protect the depositors against loss. If management and members of the board improperly use the funds of the bank for their own business ventures, the soundness of the bank is jeopardized. Any board which knowingly permits such practices is devoid of integrity.

Unsound loans to directors, their affiliates, and their friends, and illegal loans made by bank officers to businesses in which they have a substantial interest are significant causes of bank failures. Mr. Frank Wille, the Chairman of the Federal Deposit Insurance Corporation, stated that loans to directors, officers, and owners accounted for more than 50% of bank failures occurring from January, 1969, to March,

1971. If such practices are sanctioned, it is inevitable that banks will go broke. Self-interest and objectivity are antithetical.

As bank directors you should undeviatingly follow Shakespeare's admonition: "This above all: to thine own self be true." Your loans should be the best loans in the bank. They should be of such quality that other banks would instantly accept them. You should not use the power of directorship to obtain preferential terms or rates of interest.

While sending loan customers to the bank is helpful to its growth, you should not exert pressure upon bank officers to make loans. Your job is to direct, not manage.

You must not countenance the lending of bank funds by officers to business ventures in which they have more than a nominal financial interest. If you discover such a violation, you should request the board to discharge the officer; and if the board declines to take that action, you should resign immediately.

To preserve banking integrity, it is desirable that bank officers be professional, dedicated bankers—not entrepreneurs. There are several steps you can take. You should pay your officers good salaries and assure them of a decent retirement income, thereby negating the need for business "moonlighting." Bank officers should not be permitted to engage in business activities which threaten their loyalty and responsibility to the bank. You should require prior board approval for an officer to serve as a member of the board of directors of a commercial corporation.

Bank integrity directs you to keep inviolate the confidential bank information to which you are privy. Without intimating that your wife might repeat confidential banking matters, I would cite to you the conclusion of Shakesepeare's Hotspur:

> ". . . constant you are,
> But yet a woman: and for secrecy,
> No lady closer; for I well believe
> Thou wilt not utter what thou dost not know."

The people of this nation hold banks, bank officers, and bank directors to the highest standards of probity, rectitude, and integrity. If we are to enjoy public confidence, we must meet the criteria. On the cornerstone of honesty we can build for the dynamic and challenging future. As bank directors you have the duty, the responsibility, and the power to build your bank on the granite foundation of integrity.

Suggested Policy Statement

Statement of Policy

IT IS THE POLICY of the Bank that all officers and employees conduct their business affairs in such a manner and with such ethics and integrity that no conflict of interest, real or implied, could be construed. A conflict of interest shall be deemed to exist whenever an officer or employee, or a member of his immediate family, has a financial interest, direct or indirect, in a customer, supplier, or other principal dealing with the Bank, and that interest is of such extent or nature that it might reasonably affect his judgment or decisions exercised on behalf of the Bank.

The following paragraphs set forth examples of conflicts of interest, references to legal and moral restrictions, and a procedure for reporting by a Memorandum of Disclosure business interests which might be subject to criticism. Should the need arise for further clarification of the contents herein, or for discussion on any matter not mentioned, staff members should consult their appropriate senior officers.

Use of Confidential Information

Confidential or privileged information should never be used for personal advantage, or improperly divulged to anyone outside the Bank.

Outside Employment

The Bank discourages staff members from holding additional jobs outside the Bank. If, for compelling reasons, outside employment has to be sought, prior approval should be obtained from the staff member's supervising officer or Personnel department. Outside jobs must not be held if they will interfere or conflict with the interests of the Bank.

Examples of situations arising from outside employment which could involve a conflict of interest, or be subject to criticism, are:

1. Employment in activities which are competitive to the Bank.

2. Employment which involves the use of Bank equipment, supplies, or facilities.

3. Employment which involves preparation, audit, certification of statements, or documents upon which the Bank may place reliance for lending or other purposes.

4. Employment which involves rendering advice or exercising judgment which is predicated upon information, reports, or analyses, the access or availability of which results primarily from or through bank employment.

5. Employment involving a line of endeavor which is not appropriately associated with banking, or which may reflect adversely upon the bank officer or upon the Bank by way of ridicule, etc.

6. Employment under circumstances which may infer sponsorship or support of the Bank in behalf of the outside employer or an outside organization.

Borrowing and Lending Practices

Borrowing by staff members from customers of the Bank is to be limited to recognized lending institutions. Staff members are not permitted to borrow from each other.

Officers and employees should not lend personal funds to customers of the Bank other than members of their immediate families. Any exceptions are to receive prior approval of the staff member's area supervisor or department head.

Business Dealings with Customers

The Bank encourages staff members to patronize any customer engaged in legitimate professional or business activities. However, no attempt should ever be made to take personal advantage of acquaintances made or information obtained through the officer's or employee's connection with the Bank, in order to obtain special terms or price concessions.

Business Ventures with Customers

Officers and employees are not to participate in business ventures with customers without prior approval of the appropriate Executive Vice-President or of the Senior Vice-President in charge of a Division.

Personal Investments

Personal investment by a staff member or a member of his immediate family in the stock of a customer, supplier, or competitor often creates a situation where a conflict of interest could develop. Extreme care should be exercised in any such investment. And, without prior approval of the appropriate Executive Vice-President or of the Senior Vice-President in charge of a division, no officer or employee or member of his immediate family should invest in any company where the staff members' position with the Bank involves a lending or purchasing relationship with the customer.

Accepting Fees

Staff members are not permitted to accept fees from customers or businesses dealing with the Bank. This includes commissions, special discounts, or other emoluments from agencies, attorneys, insurance and real estate agents, salesmen, or others who offer such a gratuity for giving or referring business to them.

Accepting Gifts

Gifts must not be accepted from customers. This prohibition does not apply to the acceptance of items of relatively nominal value such as are sometimes given at Christmas to tellers and other public contact employees.

Acting as Broker or Agent

The Bank is not engaged in writing insurance, and it is contrary to Bank policy for any staff member to act as an insurance broker or representative. Real estate transactions, including negotiation of mortgages or trust deeds, and the sale of mortgages and trust deeds to depositors or other customers, or the making of other investments for them, as well as acting as an appraiser or an agent for collection of rents, etc., is not permitted.

Financial Speculation

Staff members should not speculate in securities, real estate, (improved or unimproved), etc., in anticipation of realizing a profit if the information which prompted the purchase of the property was gained by reason of their employment in the bank.

The rules of the Stock Exchange provide that no member of the Exchange can, "without prior consent of the employer, make a margin transaction or carry a margin account in securities or in commodities in which an employee of a bank, trust company, savings institution, insurance company, or any individual or firm engaged in the business of dealing in securities, is directly or indirectly interested."

Approval by the appropriate Executive Vice-President or by the Senior Vice-President in charge of a division is required before a staff member may have a margin account.

Fiduciary Appointments—Gifts under Wills or Trusts

Ordinarily, fiduciary appointments should be accepted by staff members only when the appointment involves estates of members of the family.

Gifts from customers of the Bank under wills or trust instruments of property, or interests in property of any kind, are not to be accepted. The fact that the staff member did not know that such a gift had been provided does not justify an exception. This prohibition does not include gifts or inheritances from members of the family.

Questions concerning this section should be referred to the appropriate Executive Vice-President or to the Senior Vice-President in charge of a division.

Fees for Negotiating Loans

The National Bank Act, 438 (c), as amended, recites as follows:

> Except as herein provided, an officer, director, employee, or attorney of a member bank who stipulates for or receives or consents or agrees to receive any fee, commission, gift, or thing of value from any person, firm, or corporation, for procuring or endeavoring to procure for such person, firm or corporation, or for any other person, firm, or corporation, any loan from or the purchase or discount of any paper, note, draft, check, or bill of exchange by such member bank shall be deemed guilty of a misdemeanor and shall be imprisoned not more than one year or fined not more than $5,000, or both.

Participation in Securities Business

Section 32 of the Banking Act of 1933, as amended by the Banking Act of 1935, provides that from and after January 1, 1936,

no officer, director, or employee of any corporation or unincorporated association, no partner or employee of any partnership, and no individual, primarily engaged in the issue, flotation, underwriting, public sale, or distribution, at wholesale or retail, or through syndicate participation, of stocks, bonds, or other similar securities, shall serve at the same time as an officer, director, or employee of any member bank except in limited classes of cases in which the Board of Governors of the Federal Reserve System may allow such service by general regulations when in the judgment of the said Board it would not unduly influence the investment policies of such member bank or the advice it gives its customers regarding investments.

Submitting Memorandum of Disclosure

The policy of the Bank requires that all situations involving a conflict of interest or a potential conflict of interest shall be disclosed. This will permit consideration of the circumstances and thereby relieve the officer or employee and the Bank of possible criticism. The procedure will be:

1. Each officer shall submit a "Memorandum of Disclosure" to the appropriate Executive Vice-President or the Senior Vice-President in charge of a division when requested, or before entering into any transaction where there is a question of possible conflict of interest.

2. Any officer knowing of any possible conflict of interest involving any employee shall request such employee to submit a "Memorandum of Disclosure."

3. Each report of any conflict of interest shall show nature of conflict, ownership or type of interest, capacity—whether direct or indirect or through immediate member of family—and all pertinent information.

4. If there is any question of a conflict of interest, the situation should be discussed with the appropriate senior officer to whom the written memorandum is to be submitted.

FRED M. PICKENS, JR.

Conflicts of Interest

BEFORE I DISCUSS the question of conflicts of interest in more general terms, let me describe a few specific situations and ask the questions they pose for the bank director.

1. Wednesday afternoon the bank loan committee, of which I am a member, met to receive a loan offering of a longtime corporate client of mine—a closely held (man and wife) corporation engaged in manufacturing metal products. The corporation, incidentally, is indebted to me for legal services over a period of about two years as a result of production falloff (a factor beyond its control), and its present bank loan is rather thinly collateralized. The corporation needed an additional advance of $25,000 for the purchase of raw materials and supplies, with a promise of expanded production and growing sales. *What should I have done?*

2. Week before last, the same loan committee met to consider an offering for a home loan. The borrower's home was being foreclosed by a small real estate investment firm owned by my law partner and myself. The applicant sought the loan to pay off the mortgage, which was being foreclosed primarily because of legal deficiency; but the proceeds would inure primarily to my real estate investment firm's benefit. *What should I have done?*

3. Only recently the XYZ corporation, in which I am a minority stockholder of five, sought a large refinancing real estate loan on its physical plant. The corporation is doing well and has good prospects for the future, but, being a seasonal business, is in need of operating capital right now. The other bank probably would have loaned it. *What should I have done?*

4. My brother-in-law is the president of one of the top five Arkansas insurance companies. He and other companies have made a pre-

sentation to my bank soliciting the bank's credit life insurance. For a long time the bank has utilized the facilities of another insurance company. The premium differential is negligible. *What should I do?*

5. I have two cousins who are both in the printing supply business. One of my cousins does business with my bank, and always has. The other does business with my competitor bank, and always has. The noncustomer printing supplier has submitted a lower bid than the customer. *What should I do?*

6. I own an option on some lots contiguous to lots held in trust by my bank. Only recently I was called in consultation with an officer of the bank for a prospective lessee of the trust lots, a highly reputable and growing chain of retail establishments. I have owned this option for some time at a nominal value because of my kinship with the owner. The option price was fixed several years ago. I know that once the information is divulged that the bank's trust lots will be leased, this property will become much more valuable. I have held the option for many years to try to put together some sort of shopping complex. *What should I do?*

7. Several months ago, one of my worst enemies, a banker in a neighboring town whom I just plain don't like, applied for a rather substantial loan on an open note with attached financial statement that would apparently justify the loan. My personal dislike made me question every item of his financial statement, for my dislike had grown to a complete mistrust of him. I admitted it to my committee colleagues. *What should I have done?*

8. Last month at my bank's discount committee meeting, a contractor friend and client of mine who sits on the board was reviewing a loan offering of a subcontractor of his with whom he has done business for many years. The subcontractor has been greatly extended and is in financial trouble. My contractor-director friend knows that if the bank does not make this loan the great probability is that he would never get the debt paid to him. *What should I do, and what should he have done?*

9. I have another brother-in-law who many years ago was my law partner. He and I have had several small business ventures together in the past. He is going to apply for an open line of credit for some of his personal undertakings. *What should I do?*

10. A doctor friend, who sits as a member of my board of directors, has recently been called upon in his capacity as director to re-

view a loan application for a group of doctors who are putting in a clinic which will be in direct competition to my doctor-director friend and his group. *What should he do?*

11. Last fall a man who owned 100 percent of the stock in a small manufacturing corporation, and with whom I had had no previous dealings except socially, approached me, ostensibly for legal counsel and advice on the possibility of retaining me to assist him in procuring a Small Business Administration loan. In the course of the conversation, however, he stated that he really felt that he could use my legal guidance and counsel as well as my very limited expertise in his field, and proposed to sell me 25 percent of the issued and outstanding stock at a much deflated value. After making this quite generous offer, and before I had had any intelligent reaction, he stated that on further thought and analysis what he felt was really needed in the business was a line of open credit at my bank for operating purposes, and that after that possibility was explored we could see about an application for an SBA loan. *What should I have done?*

12. On Christmas a year ago I was the recipient of two very handsome gifts from two personal clients of mine with whom I had had not only a very pleasant legal relationship, but a very fine personal relationship. I was deeply appreciative, but within ten days of the next year each of them, on separate occasions, called on me as a member of my bank's discount committee and as a member of the board to recommend him for a bank loan. Lo, the veil had been lifted! *What should I have done?*

Most of the above instances are factual, some are fictional. But whether fact or fiction, they, with the questions they raise, are almost daily occurrences in the life of an active director, and particularly in the life of an active outside director. If you haven't been confronted with such questions, you are not the typical outside director.

The first paragraph of the suggested policy statement on "Business Conduct—Conflict of Interest" which appears above (pp. 34-38) reads as follows:

> It is the policy of the Bank that all officers and employees conduct their business affairs in such a manner and with such ethics and integrity that *no* conflict of interest, *real or implied*, could be construed. A conflict of interest shall be deemed to exist whenever an officer or employee, or a member of his immediate family, has a financial interest, direct or indirect, in a customer, supplier, or other principal dealing with the Bank, and that interest is of *such extent or nature that it*

> *might reasonably affect his judgment or decisions exercised on behalf of the Bank.* [Emphasis supplied.]

The suggested policy statement goes on to cover many other facets of the code of conduct which should be adhered to by all officers, employees, and directors. I recommend it to you for further study and/or adoption to fit your situation.

In 1961, Mr. Sam M. Fleming, then vice-president of the American Bankers Association, in an address on "Ethics in Banking," said among other things:

> A banker should not have a financial stake in a business to which he lends money. . . . Sensible self-imposed restrictions and strict compliance with a code of ethical behaviour rather than provisions of more laws is all that is needed to lend ample protection against potential conflicts of interest situations.

Later in the same year, Homer J. Livingston, then retiring president of the Association of Reserve City Bankers, and later president and chairman of the board of the First National Bank in Chicago, in directing his remarks to a similar idea, said:

> Concern about potential conflicts of interest is stirring throughout business. . . . Questions are being increasingly asked at shareholders meetings as to what steps have been taken to determine the extent of actual or potential conflicts.

I do not believe that any bank director would deny the assertion that has been so often made: that the near fiduciary quality that characterizes most of the banker's official as well as community relationships imposes rigid moral standards on his conduct. And I would add that it is equally applicable to outside directors of banking institutions. For in the atmosphere in which we live and do business we have seen the development of the conduct of business affairs without regard to "conflict of interest," not subject to the cynosure of public eyes, until, in the 1970s (highlighted, of course, by the shocking exposures of Watergate), we are now at the point where almost every action taken by any officer and/or director, inside or outside, is to be and must be held up to the public for closer scrutiny.

This method has long since come to public commissions and public bodies under the so-called "Sunshine Laws" or Freedom of Information Acts which require public bodies to conduct all business in the open, with the news media in attendance at all deliberations. We are now entering into an era, as a result of the clamor for "full disclosure" and a demand upon the part of stockholders and customers alike, for a similar policy to become a part of the policy regulating businesses and, of course, of conducting commercial banking. We see, however, an increasing trend on the part of the government toward taking charge and writing our codes of conduct and codes of ethics. It has been well said that unless we in commercial banking write, adopt, and practice a code of conduct which is free from any taint whatsoever of conflicts of interest or the promotion of self-interest, the rash of litigation which has already sprung up over the land requiring disclosures of all transactions will be but a beginning, with superimposed bureaucratic government regulations for every transaction and activity.

Can a director take part in a decision if the other party is a company he owns? We have many cases on the point, but a recent one is the case of *Talbot* v. *James*. Mr. James, who built apartment projects to be financed with FHA insured loans, was a South Carolina president and director of Chicora Apartments. He was also sole proprietor of James Construction Company. James Construction Company got the contract to build the apartments for Chicora Apartments at a profit of $20,000, plus overhead expenses of $31,500. James got the money, received and disbursed it. Chicora got into financial difficulties, and the Supreme Court of South Carolina held that James had to return all the money to Chicora as a result of his failure to disclose to the other directors of Chicora what his interest was. In fact, the minutes did not even show that James Construction Company was to be the contractor. *Don't think for a moment that a bank director won't be held to a standard at least as high.*

More and more courts are leaning to the sound rule that every bank director should make absolutely clear to the other members of the board what his interest is, if any, in any transactions with the bank and exactly what they stand to gain personally, or for their own company, if the transaction is approved.

Should a bank make real estate loans to its directors? Any bank management would take a dim view of one of its directors going to his competitor for borrowing, and often would construe any business with a competitor bank as indicating that the director has no loyalty or confidence in his own bank. Yet there have been so many such instances of transactions with directors that were obviously favored either by repayment terms or by more favorable interest rates that we are now faced with a proposal by Chairman Wright Patman of the House Banking and Currency Committee calling for house legislation that would require all real estate loans made by a lending institution to its directors, officers, employees, and their families to be reported to the appropriate federal national regulatory body. That would make the information available to the public and to the news media.

What happened in the Westgate California Corporation matter? U.S. National Bank of San Diego, the largest bank failure in United States history, faced liability suits from almost five thousand stockholders because the board's former chairman and president took it upon himself to make loans to his corporate controlled subsidiary, Westgate California Corporation, exceeding the bank's legal limit. Though depositions have indicated that his successor as chairman had known about the loan since 1971, nothing had been done about the practice. Is there any reason to ask why more and more outside directors are demanding the purchase of liability insurance coverage, with its high premiums?

Now, let's take a gray area. All banks want outside directors to develop new business by introducing prospective borrowers to their lending officers. About ninety days ago, one of my bank board directors brought in a new resident in our city who was looking over sites and prospects for going into a new business, introduced him to the chief executive officer, and recommended him for a loan. A loan was made to him in the amount of $2,500 for the purpose of moving his family and belongings to our city, and the director even recommended the terms and suggested the interest rate (though the suggestion was not followed). Well, the man has left the city. At this moment no one knows where he is, though he came armed with good credentials. Of course the director meant well, but hell is paved with good intentions. One Kentucky bank has resolved that problem with a resolution that should any director individually attempt to influence a loan in any way, the loan officer would insist that the director endorse the loan paper personally. I offer it for your consideration. Incidentally, the director and the chief executive officer blame each other and are about half mad at each other over it.

About a year and a half ago, a holder of a rather large block of stock in a bank with which I am familiar decided, for pressing personal family reasons, to sell the stock at much below its actual value. He went to one of the executive officers, who called in a couple of directors, and they purchased it by financing the purchase through a correspondent bank at a preferential rate of interest, because of compensating balances, etc. They are now in a lawsuit brought by other stockholders and other directors, who alleged, among other things, that the inside information should have been made available to all of them, with an opportunity made to purchase the stock.

Let's go into another clearly defined area. The Policy Statement contains the following quote from the National Banking Laws:

Fees for Negotiating Loans

The National Bank Act, 438 (c), as amended, recites as follows:

> Except as herein provided, an officer, director, employee, or attorney of a member bank who stipulates for or receives or consents or agrees to receive any fee, commission, gift, or thing of value from any person, firm, or corporation, for procuring or endeavoring to procure for such person, firm, or corporation, or for any other person, firm, or corporation, any loan from or the purchase or discount of any paper, note, draft, check, or bill of exchange by such member bank shall be deemed guilty of a misdemeanor and shall be imprisoned not more than one year or fined not more than $5,000, or both.

Read this, reread it, and have your lawyer read it and explain it to you if there is any doubt in your mind.

The chairman of the board of a bank in Arkansas passed upon and approved a corporate one million dollar loan from his bank. The borrowing corporation paid a commission of $125,000 for procuring the loan to another company in which the bank board chairman held a controlling interest. On conviction of violating the FDIC Act, the board chairman argued that he did not receive the payment, although the court stated that the record clearly indicated that the payment to the bank board chairman's corporation influenced approval of the loan, saying: "Congress has clearly made it an offense for a director or officer of a Federal Deposit Insured bank to 'stipulate for' or 'receive' any fee, commission, etc., for procuring a bank loan."

In other words, no guise, no subterfuge, no cloaked conduit will serve to protect any bank officer or director who accepted in a direct or indirect manner payment in return for making the loan. Needless to add, the offending board chairman is no longer engaged in the banking business in Arkansas.

I don't mean to imply that bank directors, and especially outside ones, with all their varied business interests, should not borrow from the directors' banks. I believe that such transactions are normally in the best interests of all parties and are perfectly legal; however, if directors cause a loan to be made for their personal gain and conceal their special interests from the financial institution, they unquestionably expose themselves not only to public embarrassment, but to litigation and oftentimes prosecution. It has been suggested by the *Bank Board Letter* that the board secretary should be provided with a list of organizations, firms, and individuals with which each director has business and financial ties. Some banks have been requiring such a list on an annual basis for some time. Comptroller James Smith has spoken of such proposed regulation within the near future for national banks. I would recommend this as a policy for directors and their banks now. To face a charge of misapplication of bank funds without having such disclosure would bring down an indictment of the entire bank board.

In the 1971 session of the Arkansas legislature, the Savings and Loan Associations and the commercial banks engaged in a running battle from the opening day of the session until the closing session over what additional powers, if any, should be given to the Savings and Loan Associations, such as checking accounts, state fund depositories, commercial loan paper, etc. Happily for both sides, the matter was compromised. But in all of the many public hearings and discussions that were held, directors of many commercial banks who were also directors of Savings and Loan Associations found themselves trying to carry "water on both shoulders," though the positions taken by the two categories of financial institutions were diametrically opposite. It caused much individual embarrassment, to say the least. I ask you, *What should they have done?*– these directors who held interlocking directorates, with positions poles apart?

One of the more common difficulties that outside directors find themselves in is represented by several of the questions I posed at the inception of this talk: Are the lines of credit to outside director firms justified? Is the line more favorable than is justified by the terms other similar firms would receive from the bank? In addition to the question of conflict of interest, there arises the question of divergence of corporate opportunity and possible exposure to litigation by disgruntled shareholders of the bank. I deem it increasingly important that boards include in their minutes notations to the effect that loans made to bank officers, directors, and families of directors, as well as their businesses, were arrived at by arms-length dealings, with terms being mutually fair to lender and borrower. All of you who have had any experience as a member of a bank board will agree with me that no loans are more closely scrutinized by examining authorities than these.

I think all of us are thoroughly familiar with the problem which grew out of the Texas Gulf Sulphur cases, wherein the Circuit Court of Appeals laid down stringent guidelines for a bank "insider" or "tippee"; but now that everyone has recovered from the initial shock of the case of *SEC* v. *Texas Gulf Sulphur*, its waves are still being felt by bankers everywhere. It has been pointed out in the *Banking Law Journal* for April, 1969, that though there are many judicial decisions which are very unclear, certain guidelines can be drawn for officials who, by the nature of their business, are privy to confidential corporate information: (1) *Don't divulge it*; (2) *Don't act on it*; (3) *Don't do it*. The liability, whether "insider" or "tippee," appears now to be absolute: the restitution of profits and/or the payment of damages. The courts have gone back to one of the old legal maxims, "Where there is wrong, there is a remedy," and we see and know now that both the SEC and the courts, and probably other regulatory agencies, should and will determine, within the law, the necessary regulatory rules and restrictions to prevent such a situation's ever arising again. I would venture to say that one of the most difficult things for a director of a bank to do is to close his mind to information he has received as a director which he might in some manner utilize for his own benefit and profit. Any bank which makes a loan receives inside information. Thus, the board is privy to it. Of course, it cannot trade on that information for itself, nor can any individual director, officer, employee, or shareholder; and if it does, the bank and its directors will surely be subject to a plague of successful lawsuits.

Whatever might be the answers to all the above questions, they would probably present no problems if all affairs went smoothly. If every loan that I described in my original questions were paid off in full, it is highly doubtful that there would ever be any ultimate ill results. It is when things do not go smoothly, when affairs go wrong, and when loans are not paid that director protection is a matter of deep concern. The stock answer, "No, we did not know that," or "No, we did not do that," or "Although we could have," becomes of serious moment only when a minority stockholder has brought suit, or after serious defalcation has taken place, or after a real problem of conflict of interest has arisen, or after information thought to have been correct turns out to be incorrect. For I think each of us has observed in time of stress that if an adverse critic, a disgruntled stockholder, or a dissenting director can find deficiencies in a company's corporate procedures—*and for these practices directors are inescapably responsible*—then the directors find themselves stripped of what they thought was "protection."

Corporate records are not subject to the protective cloak of "executive privilege." The appearance of wrongdoing sometimes shakes the confidence of the public almost as much as the wrongdoing itself; so I suggest to you that if you have *any* question about whether a transaction or a matter which comes before your bank board involves any conflict of interest, resolve: first, to excuse yourself from the meeting and from the discussions, and second, abstain from voting and let the record so reflect. Oh, I know it is hard to do it. You probably know more about the quality of the matter and the prospective borrower than anybody else. But let those directors who have no possible conflict of interest pass judgment upon it.

We are living in a period of vast business as well as social and economic change. The possibilities and opportunities for conflicts of interest come most naturally to those ordinarily prominent citizens of a community who, by virtue of their character, integrity, ability, and financial standing, are most often asked to serve as members on the bank's board of directors. But that is even a stronger reason for those of us who serve on bank boards to avoid any inference of divided loyalty and/or self-dealing.

I realize that in the period of boom and prosperity through which we have been passing, the rigid principles of integrity and high sense of responsibility may seem a trifle old-fashioned, and it is often irresistible to fall subconsciously into the attitude of approaching the margin of what is right—of cutting sharp corners. And it is even easier to become so complacent and so self-satisfied that we may not be fully aware of a steady erosion of our moral and ethical responsibility as bankers and the high and significant role that the banking industry has played in the development of this country, in the elevating of living standards, in the increase of economic welfare of the people, in setting high standards for moral integrity and conscientious stewardship. But that position must never be diminished by anything less than an impeccable stewardship to those stockholders and customers who entrust their money and businesses, and oftentime their lives, to us.

Harlan Cleveland, in his little book, *The Future Executive*, one of the most thought-provoking treatises I have read in many a day, in discussing the subject that I have been covering in these remarks, says this: "Let me ask myself 'If my action is held up to public scrutiny, will I still feel that it is what I should have done, and how I should have done it?' " I agree with Mr. Cleveland: that if those involved in violating codes of ethics, those who failed to resolve conflicts of interest in the proper manner, had asked themselves this question, and answered it honestly, most of the famous instances of public corruption which have enlivened and debased our political and business history might never have happened.

Too many times directors and officers have only asked themselves: "Will I be criticized?" *This is not sufficient.* The question is: "If my action is held up to public scrutiny, will I still feel that it is what I should have done and how I should have done it?" *That alone must be the test.*

GERALD T. DUNNE

Legal Responsibilities of Bank Directors

SO MUCH HAS BEEN WRITTEN and so much has been said about the ever enlarging area of the bank director's liability as triggered by new laws and new decisions, that perhaps my keynote for this discussion should be: *Relax!* And I say so, not on my own authority, but on that of Joseph Bishop of the Yale Law School, one of our leading authorities in the area of the director, that of corporate relationships. For it was Professor Bishop who recently examined the most dramatic and seemingly perilous of these developments—two court decisions on the sweep and scope of the federal securities acts[1]—and who concluded that "[n]either decision should cause trouble for people who behave with reasonable caution and honesty and who consult their lawyers when in doubt."[2]

Now that I have begun as an amateur psychiatrist, trying to reduce levels of undue alarm to those of rational concern, let me change hats and undertake the role of historian in proposing a new tack for the examination of the legal liability of bank directors. Rather than mull over the infuriatingly uninformative formulas which the courts have developed in this area, let us go behind the scenes of the leading case, appraise its facts and its context, recast them in terms of our own times, and thereby develop a third dimension, so to speak, for a list of "dos and don'ts." On this historical field trip we will look at the range of possible legal troubles, and while our observations will try to cover the field, sins of omission rather than deliberate falls from grace will be stressed.

To begin at the beginning, however, we must take note of the deliberate falls from grace, for the simple reason that any review of the legal responsibilities of bank directors starts, not with things they have left undone, but with actions they are forbidden. More specifically, we begin with those sins of commission whose punishment is fine and imprisonment. Here we must note seven federal criminal statutes[3] which can have an application to bank directors as such. These seven deadly sins are: (1) embezzlement, (2) making false entries, (3) taking fees for making loans, (4) tendering loans or gratuities to bank examiners, (5) false certification of checks, (6) making political contributions with bank funds, and (7) borrowing from trust funds.

Perhaps we can add an eighth deadly sin, for the federal bank robbery statutes technically covers anybody who goes into a bank with the intention of committing a federal crime—not necessarily robbery—therein.[4]

These laws should be noted at the outset for two reasons. First, we are told by an old French proverb that things which go without saying should always be said; hence in any discussion of the responsibilities of bank directors these statutes must be mentioned. Second, they must be mentioned not only to suggest compliance with their letter, but to exhort fulfillment of their spirit. That is to say that, in these areas, a bank director must emulate Caesar's wife and be above suspicion. Here of all places he must turn square corners and avoid any situation in which any possible brush with the law could arise. Here are two examples: Should a bank director encounter bank examiners in a restaurant in his town, he must suppress any impulse to ask the waitress for their check. Far from extending an amenity, such impulsive generosity is only starting something which at best can be but an embarrassment to all parties concerned. Again, every bank director should always remember that the crime of making false entries covers any deliberately deceitful entry in the bank's records, however benign the motive, and the intention to harm the bank—that is, to take its money—is not necessarily a part of the offense.

From these forbidden actions, wrong in themselves and prohibited at all times, we move to an area where the legal consequences of what a director does are determined not by content but by circumstance. There is nothing wrong in itself in making a well-secured million-dollar loan to a responsible borrower whose business, circumstances, and prospects warrant such a credit. In fact, that is what banks are for. But it is very wrong if the bank's loan limit is $500,000. Or again, it is even worse, whatever the loan limit, if a bank director holds a financial interest in the borrower, yet proceeds to work both sides of the street in self-dealing and self-effrontery by asking for a loan in one capacity and approving it in the other.

The first situation concerns that variety of constraints of which loan limits are the principal and perhaps the characteristic concern, but by no means the only one. Here violation typically entails civil rather than criminal liability, and it can run to a substantial magnitude. Thus, a director who approves a loan above an amount a bank may legally lend a single borrower may be held liable, not merely for the excess portion, but for the entire amount of the credit. Hence, while these positive restrictions may not necessarily involve criminal sanctions, their range of civil liability is formidable and should be carefully noted and studied.

In an entirely different category are those constraints of the second type which forbid self-dealing and self-serving. Here one does not need a long list of "don'ts" but only a conscience of average sensitivity. Here the law is built on the basis of experience, and that experience continues to unfold. In fact, we will shortly look at what we have most recently learned from it—that a misuse of information to one's personal gain is not distinguishable in principle from a corresponding misuse of property to the same end. For irrespective of details, all such betrayals of trust can run counter to that injunction of the law which an Australian law teacher called "puritan in its inflexibile morality."[5] They are subject to legal redress, which may take the form of monetary damages in a civil suit or ouster from office, and may also involve, worst of all, loss of reputation and esteem.

This lengthy, but unavoidable, preliminary brings us to what is in any practical context the major area of the director's legal responsibility, for we have been looking at deliberate crimes and their next-door neighbors, deliberate self-serving and deliberate self-seeking, merely to lay them aside. These are self-evident grounds for legal liability. Rather, the director's true concern must come in an area with a less obvious focus: What should be the guidelines for a man of good faith and limited knowledge who has a crowded schedule and therefore must of necessity leave the operation of the bank to others?

Basically, the law is divided on this question, offering two answers.[6] Both propose something of a rule of reason, but with very different consequences. One rule, enunciated by the Supreme Court for directors of national banks and largely followed by most states as to banks chartered under their authority and representing the weight of authority, we can call the "reasonable directors" test. The other, a minority view, can be labeled the "personal affairs" test. The first asserts that a director must give such attention to his bank as is reasonable under the circumstances. The other proposes that a director give the same amount of attention as would be reasonable in the conduct of his personal business.

If the reader feels that these rules tell him little, and that perhaps under certain circumstances he cannot even tell the rules apart, he has company. On the other hand, the United States Supreme Court and virtually every state court which has examined the matter in the light of the hard facts of specific controversies have had to recognize and apply one rule or the other. We should remember, however, that neither rule was handed to us engraved on tablets of stone. Rather, both are responses to environment, shaped by circumstances, and pointed toward achieving certain results. Both are end products of discoveries, analogies, and restatements. And both were formulated within a historical context which saw the tactical day-to-day control of corporations shift successively from the owners to the board of directors to management. This is still an ongoing process, the current developments of which should be a source of concern, but hardly of alarm.

A good enough place to begin is the case of *Wood* v. *Dummer,*[7] decided in 1824, which involved a liquidating dividend in violation of the rights of creditors. In deciding that the payment might follow into the hands of the stockholders, Justice Joseph Story of the United States Supreme Court brilliantly blended the ancient law of trusts and the evolving law of business corporations. He ruled, in effect, that corporate property was a trust fund, that corporate creditors and shareholders were beneficiaries, and that directors were trustees.

A trustee's distinguishing characteristic is, of course, that he holds legal title to property for the benefit of another, and accordingly, Justice Story's analogy held a particular application in the case of banks precisely because they differ from other businesses in this specific respect. And not only do banks do business almost wholly with other people's money, but it is money which has been either directly or by implication brought to the bank through the use of the directors' names. Moreover, a bank must stand ready to pay out that money to the penny and on very short notice. As a consequence, banks are quite different from other businesses. In the first place, banking is a business of restricted entry, with an enormous burden of proof of public need and financial responsibility being laid on those wishing to start a bank. Once underway, a bank cannot be allowed to undergo the rigors of what is otherwise routine business competition, wherein a premium is placed on chance-taking and the losers are penalized by failure and collapse. The failure of a bank penalizes the banker, to be sure, but it also visits his sins upon the heads of his customers and his entire community. For this reason, a bank operates within a vast web of legal restraints; there are restrictions on where it does business, when it does business, what assets it may acquire, how much it may loan, how much it may invest, what interest it can charge, what interest it can pay, and so on and so on. And, significantly, compliance with these constraints is enforced by a pattern of continuing disclosure, largely through the visits of examiners who arrive unannounced, unexpected, and quite possibly unwanted. The examiners ask a great many questions. Their work necessarily involves interference in operations. They may, from time to time, meet with the Board of Directors.

And this mention of the office of directors not only brings us back to the director's special responsibility, but also suggests another dimension in which banks differ from other businesses. For if we place certain provisions of the National Banking Act (or virtually any state banking act) and certain cognate statutes alongside the model corporation code, some striking differences immediately emerge:

1. Bank directors take an oath of office; nonbank directors do not.

2. Bank directors have residence and citizenship requirements; nonbank directors do not.

3. Certain occupations involving successful and honorable men are barred from bank boards. There is no general parallel in other businesses.

4. A bank director must own some stock. Again, the parallel condition does not exist in nonbanking firms.

5. A bank director's conduct of his affairs may result in his being subject to a cease-and-desist order, or quite possibly even being separated from his office by public authority. This is a sword of Damocles without analogy in general business.

In short then, this formidable battery of laws which deal with the selection, the qualification, and the tenure of bank directors makes it abundantly clear that this is a deadly serious business. It is an office not of honor but of service, in which disinterest, diligence, and prudence are to be the rule. If there is the opposite, if indeed instead of diligence, disinterest, and prudence, we have self-serving, negligence, inattention, or recklessness, then there is the legal consequence of unfulfilled responsibility—legal liability.

So at the heart of the matter are the questions: What are the bank director's yardsticks and guidelines? What exact dos and don'ts must be observed? What are the specific guidelines? And the answer is that there are none, at least none in the hard-and-fast sense of a thirty-mile-an-hour speed limit. There are none for two opposing reasons. On the one hand, courts have explicitly refused to lay an undue burden upon desirable men who would otherwise be willing to serve as directors. On the other, they have—to borrow a phrase from former Chairman Cohen of the SEC—refused to establish "standards for the sharp shooters to evade."[8]

The best exposition, and indeed the reasons for the standards (or more precisely, the lack of them) was enunciated in the landmark case of *Briggs* v. *Spaulding.*[9] It was a relatively simple lawsuit. A receiver of a national bank sued its directors to recover losses on the grounds that they had paid no attention to the affairs of the bank, had failed to hold or call meetings, or appoint a committee for examination, or make a personal examination, but had allowed the executive officers to manage without supervision. The immediate cause of the loss was the misfeasance of the bank's chief executive, a man with a reputation of trustworthiness and efficiency, but one who had, in fact, mismanaged the institution into insolvency. There was no question as to the honesty of the directors. The issue concerned their diligence in serving a bank where theory and practice had diverged considerably.

In theory and on paper there were reassuring provisions, for the bank's by-laws provided for monthly meetings of the board and the semi-annual appointment of a director's examination committee. In fact, however, no committee was appointed for at least fourteen years, and board meetings themselves were infrequent and perfunctory. If the board was below its own mark, however, some compensation could be found in the chief executive, a brilliant young man who had gone into the bank as a messenger boy and in fourteen years had advanced to the top job. He came from a fine local family, was treasurer of a leading church and an officer of the YMCA, and was otherwise engaged in civic and charitable good works. "His general character was good, his reputation for integrity and financial capacity excellent, and he possessed the confidence of his fellow citizens." Moreover, he owned two-thirds of the stock of the bank. About four months after assuming active management he asked two outstanding local citizens, one a lawyer and the other a businessman, to go on the board. Both were older men and the lawyer, an ex-congressman, by singular coincidence had played a part in the passage of the National Banking Act.

The responses of both were not unusual. The businessman demurred on the grounds that he lacked knowledge of the banking business and that his own affairs took him out of town for considerable periods. Finally, upon being informed that the bank was in prosperous condition and that not much of his time would be required, he accepted. However, his wife became ill shortly thereafter and he himself came under a strain which incapacitated him for general attendance to business.

The attorney's case was somewhat similar. He was seventy-two years old, was the honorary president of a leading bank, and was connected with several financial corporations. Retired from business, he gave little attention to the affairs of his own bank; but looking on himself as something of an elder statesman, he was willing to give such advice or counsel as might be requested.

During the time the brilliant young man held executive control of the bank the directors met only twice, contrary to the explicit requirement of the by-laws for monthly meetings. One of the two meetings was for the purpose of passing resolutions relative to the death of a former officer. The second was to put the two defendants on the board. The extent of their supervision seems to have been characterized by a casual visit by one of them who chatted and asked how things were going. Needless to say, the answer was "nicely." On the assurance of the chief executive, the other went even farther and actually signed a fraudulent statement of condition without having the slightest knowledge of its truth or falsity.

Then, three months after their appointment, disaster struck. The bank was examined, and the examiner discovered that its liabilities exceeded its assets because of uncollectable and illegal credits arising out of the chief executive officer's outside business interests. There was no contention that the directors knew, much less condoned, this unhappy tangle; but on the assumption that they had been negligent in permitting the events to happen, the receiver of the bank sued to recover the losses.

The receiver lost in the lower tribunal, and the case wound up in the Supreme Court, where in a five-to-four decision Justice Harlan, grandfather of the present justice, wrote a blistering dissenting opinion in which he said: "In fact, those gentlemen, while they were directors, had no knowledge whatever of what was being done by (the chief executive) in the conduct of the bank. They took his word that all was right, and gave no attention whatever to the management of its business."[10]

As to the lawyer and ex-congressman, Justice Harlan was particularly severe:

> It is plain from the evidence that if, with his long experience in banking business, he had given one hour, or at the utmost a few hours time, in any week, while he was a director, to ascertain how this bank was being managed, he would have discovered enough that was wrong and reckless to have saved the [bank], its stockholders and its depositors, many, if not all, the losses, thereafter occurring. Upon his theory of duty, the only need for directors of a national bank is to meet, to take the required oath of administering its business honestly and diligently, to turn over all its affairs to the control of one or more of its officers, and never go near the bank again, unless they are notified to come there or until they are informed that there is something wrong. . . . No bank can be safely administered in that way. Such a system cannot be properly characterized otherwise than as a farce. It cannot be tolerated without peril to the business interests of the country.[11]

Now it must be emphasized that the foregoing was the *dissenting* opinion which proposed a theory which was *not* adopted. While Justice Harlan did not say so, he was in fact getting close to the so-called "personal affairs" test, which is to say that a bank director must give the bank something of the same time, care, and attention that a reasonable man would give his own business, where he would have both the time to do so and an intimate knowledge of operating details. Or to put the matter another way, he proposed a fairly rigorous application of Justice Story's trustee analogy. However phrased, his proposal was rejected, and the rejection emphasizes how much the courts have been willing to give honest directors the benefit of the doubt. Moreover, the dissent serves as a backdrop for the appreciation of the majority opinion which, on this point, represents the weight of authority in American law.

For it was the opposite theory, "the reasonable director" test, which, while not labeled as such, was adopted by the majority of the Court and was epitomized by one sentence in the majority opinion: ". . . Conduct [of directors] is to be judged, not by the event, but by the circumstances under which they acted." What is the underlying basis of this rule? The answer is in both law and history. Justice Story's trustee rule worked in New England in 1820 when directors directed in the most literal sense; and no matter, however small, such as ordering the clerk to start an early fire on meeting days or buying a lock from the state prison, was beneath the formality of motion, second, and entry in the minutes. It could not work in an environment where operational control had gravitated to management and where the director had become a part-time official concerned only with policy. This development occurred on both sides of the Atlantic, and in fact it was from a quotation of English precedent that the Supreme Court took its decision in *Briggs* v. *Spaulding*—that any other rule (including, obviously, the personal affairs test) would "deter all men of any property, and perhaps all men who have any character to lose from becoming directors of companies at all."[12] The Court went further yet and said it would not lay down as a rule that there is an invariable presumption of rascality as to the officers and employees. In fact, it again quoted precedent that: ". . . no law . . . requires . . . directors . . . to adopt a system of espionage . . . [Officers] must be supposed to act honestly until the contrary appears; and the law does not require their employers to entertain . . . suspicions without some apparent reason."[13]

Hence, the Court refused to come up with a yardstick. Instead, it delivered itself of a maddeningly imprecise, and yet—considering the facts of the foregoing case—a most reassuring opinion. Modifying but not completely rejecting Justice Story's equation of directors and trustees, the Court held:

> It is perhaps unnecessary to defend the degree of care and prudence which directors must exercise in the performance of their duties. The degree of care required depends upon the subject to which it is to be applied, and each case has to be determined in view of all the circumstances. They are not insurers of the fidelity of the agents whom they have appointed, who are not their agents but the agents of the corporation; and they cannot be held responsible for losses resulting from the wrongful acts or omissions of other directors or agents, unless the loss is a consequence of their own neglect of duty, either for failure to supervise the business with attention or in neglecting to use proper care in the appointment of agents.[14]

The holding has been severely criticized. Professor Bishop, whom I quoted at the beginning, called it the "most notorious example of judicial indulgence."[15] And more than that, we have the word of Learned Hand, surely one of our greatest judges, that had *Briggs* v. *Spaulding* been tried in his day, the judgment "probably would have gone the other way."[16]

Judge Hand did not say, however, that the minority view of "personal affairs" test would be imposed. Indeed, given the constraints of time, memory, and energy, this would mean that a man *could* serve on but one board of directors—at most. Rather, the judge really affirmed the *Briggs* v. *Spaulding* test, contending that it all depends on the circumstances, and the circumstances having changed—particularly in business ethics, sensitivity, and concerns—so did the result.

More to the point perhaps, even *Briggs* v. *Spaulding* said that a director's responsibility involved more than officiating as a figurehead. And that is a good point of beginning. For while officiating implies, obviously, more than regular physical presence at board meetings, physical presence itself is the indispensable beginning. Indeed, a director can get in more trouble by staying away than he can by showing up, for absence, like ignorance, is no excuse. Quite to the contrary, a director's liability is joint and several, which to say that each man implicitly underwrites his colleagues, and he does so both when he is with them and when he is away from them.

But he should be with them, and that is the very reason there are residence requirements. If a director cannot see his way clear to attend the meetings of his board regularly, he should not accept appointment; or if this situation intervenes after appointment, he should resign. Even more to the point, his attendance should be an informed and intelligent one, *and the record should show it.* It is up to him whether the board minutes can be used as Plaintiff's Exhibit A or Defendant's Exhibit No. 1 in some subsequent lawsuit. And this concern with the record should run to the *whole* record—that is to say he should insist on receiving information about the bank in concise, meaningful, and written form when it is not furnished that way as a matter of course.

This concern involves at least three consequences. First, it implies the necessity of an ongoing check of the integrity not only of specific information furnished, but of the system that supplies it. For whatever might have been the standards of accountancy and audit in the days of *Briggs v. Spaulding*, the world has come a long way since then. In the last part of the twentieth century this means not only an independent check to assure the valuation of the bank's assets, but a recording of its liabilities. It also means a concern with systems and procedures which meet the classic threefold test of keeping temptation from the weak, opportunity from the venturesome, and suspicion from the innocent. It means a concern that the bank examinations shall not be exercises in futility, but rather shall be valuable sources of admonition, intelligence, and insight. And it means a concern with the legal framework within which the bank must operate. This does not mean that directors must become lawyers or examiners. But it does mean that they satisfy themselves that the bank has able counsel—and I would say your legal fees are one of the biggest bargains you can have—and it also means an intelligent general knowledge of the general ground rules on loans, investment, capital, and dividends.

Thus all the foregoing can be summarized and the director's responsibility expressed in a single word—information. From this critical point, the rest of his job unfolds as either prelude or effect, and fulfills that old adage: Take care of the penny and the dollars will take care of themselves. Any director who stays up on the basic statistics of his job—resources, capital, loan-deposit ratio, deposit mix, liquidity ratio, general portfolio composition, loan limits, employee turnover—has taken the first and indispensable step in vindicating it.

To be sure, there is more to information than tactical data. The background material also has its critical place, and here I refer to what I might call the director's textbooks. Here there is almost an embarrassment of riches, so I will mention but two—the American Bankers Association's *The Bank Director*, and that admirable compendium of the Comptroller of Currency, *Duties and Liabilities of Directors of National Banks*. Finally, there is the all-important duty of keeping generally informed in the area of public affairs. Along this line a superb briefing in current banking events can be had merely by scanning the *American Banker* every morning. Another wonderful bird's-eye view is afforded by the business and financial summary on the front page of the *Wall Street Journal*.

Thus, any bank director who follows the financial press will have picked up very early in the game what is currently perhaps the most topical aspect of his job, and this is the necessity of assuring that confidential information is appropriately safeguarded. It is an old duty, but it has received recent emphasis in the *Texas Gulf Sulphur*, *Douglas Aircraft* and *Bar Chris* cases. For these cases can be seen as extensions of the basic fiduciary aspects of the director's job to new but nonetheless logical dimensions. Moreover, they have especial application to bank directors, for whom the handling of other people's money and the handling of the details of other people's business are obviously closely related. Hence, one of the early stories on the "insider" controversy was headlined: "Warning the Bankers Found in Douglas Probe."[17] Its gist was expressed in a single sentence:

> One banker last week, suddenly realizing that the restraints on management use of inside information have been tightened and the definition of insiders is now covering a great number of individuals, asserted, "I think I will call a board meeting for tomorrow and bring in our public relations man to warn everybody about the potential liability."

And following shortly thereafter came another story, "SEC Rule on 'Insider Information' Applies to Bank,"[18] reporting the statement of the then chairman of the SEC to the effect that bankers are subject to certain SEC enforcement of antifraud provisions of the securities legislation, notwithstanding their supervision by other agencies.

What the exact line of advance of this development will be is by no means clear, so we must await the usual process of legal growth and distinction. What has resulted, however, is a renewed interest in the so-called directors' and officers' liability insurance, sometimes popularly known as D & O. The purchase of D & O by banks and other corporations has been authorized in a variety of enactments, regulations, and interpretations. So by all means look into this insurance, and equally important, have your counsel look into it. Do read the literature of the carriers and the other material which has been written on the subject, and then make your own informed decision. For if your decision is informed, it will include two elements. One is that there are some liabilities against which no one can protect you, save yourself. And the other is that, even as to insurable liability, coverage is no substitute for competence and care. For just as your conduct with respect to smoking should be the same regardless of the fire coverage on your house, and just as your driving habits should be unrelated to the insurance on your car, so your conduct as a director, that is to say the diligent vindication of the oath you took, should not be contingent upon insurance or the lack of it.

For in the final analysis the choice between legal liability and legal safety is yours alone. No insurer, no fellow director, no elected officer can make it for you. And—to return to my opening theme—it is an easy choice and one automatically made by a director whose behavior is characterized by caution, honesty, and consultation with counsel when in doubt. I do hope that your own decision will be so made.

Notes

1. SEC v. Texas Gulf Sulphur Co., 401 F. 2d 833 (1968) and Escott v. Bar Chris Corp., 283 F. Supp. 643 (1868).
2. "Protecting Corporate Insiders," *Review of Securities Regulation* 28 (1969): 945. Professor Bishop is the coauthor with Judge George T. Washington of *Indemnifying the Corporate Executive* (1963) and numerous periodical articles on directors' liability.
3. See 18 USC 656, 1005, 215, 212, 1004, 591, and 12 USC 92a(h).
4. 18 USC 2113; see also Jerome v. United States, 318 U.S. 101 (1943).
5. Ross W. Parsons, "The Director's Duty of Good Faith," *Melbourne University Law Review* 5 (1967): 396.
6. Rudolph Zeiger, Jr., "Liability of Corporate Directors," *Dickenson Law Review* 71 (1967): 668.
7. Federal Cases #17, 944 (1824).
8. Quoted in *American Banker*, December 6, 1968.
9. 141 U.S. 132 (1891).
10. 141 U.S. at 166.
11. Id. at 168-69.
12. Id. at 149.
13. Id. at 162.
14. Id. at 147.
15. "Sitting Ducks and Decoy Ducks," *Yale Law Journal* 77 (1967): 1097.
16. Barnes v. Andrews, 298 F. at 616 (1934).
17. *American Banker*, September 3, 1968.
18. Id., December 6, 1968.

ROBERT H. FABIAN

Some of the Legal Responsibilities Of Bank Directors

THERE IS a fairly well-developed body of law defining the legal responsibilities of those persons who have been elected directors of banks. A part of the law is statutory, the sources being legislative enactments of the United States Congress and the several states. These statutory guidelines have been amplified and implemented by rulings and regulations issued by regulatory authorities, such as the Comptroller of the Currency, the FDIC, the Federal Reserve Board, the several state superintendents of banks, and the SEC.

Some of these statutes are criminal in nature, imposing fines and imprisonment for willful violations. Others merely establish duties, the violation of which may result in the issuance of cease and desist orders, removal from office, or even forfeiture of the bank's charter. Violations which damage the bank may also provide grounds for a stockholder's derivative suit against the director, seeking money damages. For example, in Illinois a judgment was recently entered against a director-president of a bank for about $99,000 in damages arising from charged-off loans which the defendant had authorized in excess of the bank's 10% lending limit. Understandably, following reports of this decision, bank directors in Chicago and other places throughout the nation became more concerned with questioning whether or not the bank's management was conforming to the 10 percent lending limit and related regulations. Some became aware of the 10 percent limit for the first time.

Another part of the law finds its roots in cases decided by the courts, both federal and state. Still other guidelines, rules, and principles find their roots in generally accepted moral concepts such as integrity, honesty, fairness, and ethics. It is apparent, therefore, that there is no shortage of source material on the subject. The problem, rather, is to isolate and emphasize those items which are most important.

The isolation of specific problems and areas of responsibilities has become more and more difficult in the last few years because exquisite new dimensions have been added by the bank holding company phenomenon and the popularity of class actions which bring into sharp focus alleged abuses on the part of corporate management. The holding company phenomenon becomes important because many bank directors have now become members of the boards of nonbank corporations, thus subjecting themselves to the impact of the laws governing the conduct of directors and insiders of general business corporations. In other words, the scope of the impact of the law upon a director's job is substantially broadened if a directorship of a nonbank corporation, such as a holding company, is also undertaken.

The statutes clearly vest in the board of directors of a bank the general power of management of the bank, with an implied power to delegate day-to-day operations to selected officers. The basic responsibility for management and compliance with the laws cannot, however, be delegated; it remains with the members of the board, both as individuals and as a group.

The basic standards of conduct of a director are not much different for the director of a bank than they are for the director of any other business corporation. Characteristically, the statutes provide that the business and affairs of a corporation "shall be managed by a board of directors." This is a statement so universal that it is almost impossible to deal with it in real life, because even though the statutes direct a board to manage the corporate affairs, the fact is that they cannot do so in any corporation of large or medium size. As Tex Thornton, the chairman of Litton Industries, puts it, a board of directors should not stray into the management function, because "if it does, you run the danger of ending up with committee management on a part-time basis, and nothing could be more disastrous."

We must turn, therefore, to the case law, where we find two principles enunciated. The first is the requirement that directors serve with loyalty to the interests of stockholders—a requirement which precludes their making individual profits at the expense of stockholders. This guideline is quite clear and need not detain us.

The second principle is less of a solution than it appears to be. It is that directors have a responsibility to exercise prudent business judgment; but in doing so, they will not be held liable for mistakes of judgment that result in a loss. The statutory language articulating this duty in most states reads as follows:

> Directors and members of any committee designated by the board shall discharge their duties in good faith and with that degree of diligence, care and skill which ordinarily prudent men would exercise under similar circumstances in like positions.

The duties, therefore, are those of loyalty and prudence.

The questions then become, (a) what would an ordinarily prudent man do in order to demonstrate the exercise of his characteristic diligence, care, and skill, and (b) are there any guidelines or limitations? Most frequently, the statutes provide that a director is not liable if he acted in good faith on financial statements offered by the appropriate officer of the corporation or an independent public accountant. For example, the Texas statute provides that a director may safely rely upon the written opinion of the attorney for the corporation. The Oklahoma statutes do not mention the attorney, but they provide that a director may safely rely upon the financial statements offered by a corporate officer or by a certified public accountant.

The reliance must be in good faith, which means that the report or records may not provide protection if their substance is such as to tax credulity, or if the mode of expression is such as to suggest some question as to candor and completeness as judged by the standards of the reasonable man.

This leads to consideration of what steps a director should take to increase his sophistication so that he can consistently act as would the prudent man "under similar circumstances in like positions." At the outset, it seems to me that the director must demonstrate an acquaintance with the business background of the corporation. This presupposes some business educational background or experience and a curiosity and awareness as to what really is going on.

It is sometimes said that boards of directors are created to decide broad questions of policy. As a matter of fact, in most instances, matters of broad policy do not come before the board of directors until legal or societal forces have become so strong that they will permit only one answer. For example, the question of whether a corporation will take steps to protect the environment has already been answered by the National Environmental Policy Act, which directs that the regulatory agencies enforce compliance with strict standards. Mr. J. M.

Roche has said: "General Motors *responds* to society's expectations."

A second approach is advocated by E. Everett Smith of McKinsey & Co.: that directors should perform or, at least, commission "an audit of management quality." At first blush this appears to be a safe statement, but upon analysis it seems that if a board of directors went snooping around the ranks of management, either the board would not be tolerated for long or good management would leave. There are ways, however, in which directors can inform themselves so that they will be in a position to assess the basic capability and dependability of individuals in management. This includes at the least the duty of appraising the personal honesty and ability of the top ranks of management, and encouraging opportunities to see the officers of the bank or corporation and to hear them report. Much can be learned by looking at a person and listening to him answer a question or make a statement or a presentation.

A third approach may prove even more productive in the fulfillment of the good-faith requirement. A director must be able to prove, according to the standard of the Securities Act, that he had, after reasonable investigation, reasonable ground to believe, and did believe, that the statement was true and complete. The concept of reasonable investigation embodied in this text means that the director must have some time to ponder the relevant information before he must make a decision. This means that directors should have adequate and seasonal information before voting. One way which has been found helpful in some corporations which have outside directors is to assign to a bank officer the duty of attending policy meetings of the managerial group and communicating their tone and substance to the full board. This is a sensitive and delicate assignment, and in medium and small size banks it should probably be given to a person who has the full trust and confidence of the chief executive officer.

All of this boils down to the inescapable responsibility of directors to see that management is doing its job. The wise choice of capable management and the removal of management that fails the responsibility are the central and culminating responsibilities of the board. Where there is no trust one of the two must go, and it is better if management is made to leave.

The responsibility for management carries with it several rather well-defined duties about which there is little argument or difficulty. Some of these duties are the wise selection of honest and capable executive officers to manage the day-to-day affairs of the bank within the policy framework established by the board. The duties extend not only to the initial selection, but also to a continuous surveillance of the management in order to detect deterioration at an early stage. Surveillance includes observance of personal habits to detect early signs of addiction to alcohol, drugs, horses, dice, or indiscriminate expensive consorting with women not their wives.

This responsibility is carried out by regular attendance and active participation in board meetings, by preparation in advance of board meetings of appropriate areas of inquiry, and by aggressive inquiry into the affairs of the bank. There is a duty to inquire beyond the items which are formally placed on the agenda by the managing officers. In my view, each director attending a meeting should have his own hidden agenda which he develops by himself. Questions have a beneficial psychological effect on management, even if they seem to some to be superficial or unimportant. I recognize that carrying out this suggestion may tend to discourage the normal atmosphere of good fellowship and camaraderie that is customary at board meetings. Nobody very much enjoys playing the role of the wart on the wings of progress or the meddlesome negative member. But an attitude of mild suspicion on the part of the directors creates a most healthful attitude on the part of the management. Human nature being what it is, there is often a tendency on the part of bank management to be less than candid in discussing the problems confronting the bank, since we all enjoy praise much more than criticism.

I would also inquire about vacations and insist that they be taken by officers for continuous periods of at least two weeks each year, because many important defalcations are discovered when an officer or employee is forced to be away. In some European countries, and to some extent here, the manager or executive is replaced by an auditor-type for two or three consecutive weeks each year. Of course, directors also have a duty to see to it that the bank is adequately protected by fidelity bonds and that action is taken to collect aggressively the monies owed to the bank. Directors should insist that lawsuits be filed to collect charged-off loans. The publicity will not be adverse. Inquiries into these subjects are also recommended.

All of these suggestions may be remembered if you accept the premise that people do what you *in*spect, not what you *ex*pect.

A bank's board is no place for a shill director who must be loved by all of the people all of the time. Each director should risk his position to the extent of brinksmanship if he is to contribute properly to the welfare of the bank and discharge his trust. In this context, being most negative often amounts to being most positive. But, of course, the line must be drawn short of conduct which is destructive of the self-confidence of your officers, or which is overly time-consuming and boring.

Directors have a general civil liability, and sometimes a liability to criminal penalties if they *knowingly* permit the bank to engage in violation of the governing laws and their implementing regulations. This includes the Federal Reserve Act, the National Bank Act, the Glass-Steagall Act, the various securities acts, the antitrust laws, and some others of lesser importance. Excellent discussions of these are contained in a booklet, now in its thirteenth edition, reprinted from the *Journal of the American Bankers Association.*

The question of what is a *knowing* violation of one of the rules and regulations is worthy of some attention. Under the cases that have been brought, a director who is totally ignorant of the facts involving the violation may still be chargeable with knowledge of it. A director is chargeable with knowledge if he has failed to inquire adequately, even though he may attend meetings regularly. He may be chargeable with knowledge of a violation that occurs in his absence, if his attendance habits are poor. He may be chargeable with knowledge if he attends the meetings and sleeps. He is probably not chargeable if he has become senile. But if he has become obviously senile, there is a duty on the part of the other directors to seek his removal from the board.

A director is subject to certain criminal penalties if he knowingly permits the bank's books to contain false and misleading entries, or if he knowingly permits the making of loans to bank examiners or permits the bank to make political contributions. The Hatch Act and the Corrupt Practices Act, which are federal statutes, are applicable both to federally chartered institutions and to state chartered institutions insured by the FDIC.

Other examples in which criminal liability may be imposed upon a director for knowingly violating the statutes and regulations are the approving of loans which do not conform to the margin requirements set by Regulation U of the Federal Reserve Board and, of course, the permitting of indirect payment of interest on demand deposits in violation of Regulation Q. In a recent New York case the court held that the bank which had made a loan in violation of Regulation U could not collect the total amount of the debt from the broker-borrower, the ground of that decision being that the bank knew that the transaction was for the special purpose of carrying listed stocks, and it was thus frustrating the public policy of the Act and the Regulation.

There are broader considerations, some of which are not directly related to banks, but are implicit in the position of any corporate director. All of these responsibilities can be grouped under general concepts of fairness, integrity, and honesty. The acceptance of a position as a bank director inevitably carries with it the necessity for proper resolution of conflicts of interest. The temptation to mishandle such conflicts is greater in smaller, closely held banks than in big ones.

Potential conflicts of interest exist in almost every transaction. For example, many banks have outside directors on their boards who are engaged in business and who are affiliated with corporations or partnerships requiring the use of the bank's facilities. In such instances, the other directors and the borrowing director have a duty to see to it that, for the protection of the stockholders, transactions are kept at arms length and are fair to both sides, and that executive interference with decisions normally entrusted to management at lower levels is not indulged.

Sometimes business opportunities become available which might be placed with the bank, or placed in another entity in which divergent groups of insiders have varying interest. A business opportunity which comes to a director as a result of his directorship belongs to the bank, and the bank should have the first opportunity to take advantage of it. This situation occurs when a bank director is also a director of other corporations having business relationships with the bank.

There is no pat formula for resolving the conflicts of interest which will inevitably arise except the development of an awareness that conflicts will arise, that divided loyalties do exist, and that they can only be resolved in an atmosphere of high integrity, under tests of fairness, candor, and honesty. If conscience has become an outmoded concept, you may substitute a publicity test as a guideline. You can, for example, ask yourself whether you would be embarrassed if what you did and your motivation for doing it were to be published in tomorrow morning's newspaper. If you would be embarrassed, the chances are that the conflict has not been properly resolved.

During the past year, there has been a revival of the debate as to whether bank directors and bank management are permitted to devote portions of the earning assets to projects which appear to result in maximizing the earnings of the bank for the short-range benefit of the stockholders. For example, should a bank buy sewer bonds delivering a smaller yield because it is motivated to improve the water quality of the nearby streams? I believe this question can readily be resolved by comparing long-range and short-range benefits to the stockholders. For example, if the health and environment of the community which the bank serves is dependent upon immediate steps being taken to stop pollution, and if the bank expects to survive and grow with the community, it seems to me that the bank management quite wisely might determine that it must sacrifice short-term yields so that the community may remain livable and grow and prosper. If the public improvement is necessary, the long-range benefits will far outweigh the short-term sacrifice. Therefore, I think it is perfectly legal for a board knowingly to sacrifice a portion of a dividend payout or even short-term earnings for the benefit of the long view.

A sensitivity to the market price of your stock, if it is widely held, or to the grumblings of the larger stockholders if it is not, will quickly reveal whether you have sacrificed too much in the interest of the public weal to the detriment of immediate cash flow to your stockholders.

So far I have touched generally upon danger areas, and I am afraid I have painted a dim picture of the bank director's job. There are, however, some duties which give comfort. For example, a director is not an insurer that each loan that the bank makes will be collectible. His legal responsibility is that he exercise in good faith his best business judgment, acting as a prudent man in the same or similar circumstances. The prudent man in a directorship will, if he has no special knowledge of the banking business, take the trouble to get some knowledge and experience of it.

If you do not feel like continuing to assume these responsibilities without insurance of your personal fortunes, there are three other things which you can do:

1. Examine the bylaws of your institution to see to it that they contain appropriate indemnification provisions protecting against liability or threatening liability for mistakes in judgment, stopping short of criminal or dishonest acts.

2. Insurance can be purchased which will cover a director's liabili-

ty for exposures which are not indemnifiable. For example, a stockholder may sue in a derivative action filed on behalf of the bank seeking damages which would benefit all stockholders. Such a judgment could not be reimbursed by the bank. Many banks have purchased such insurance for the benefit of their directors, and the existence of such a policy seems to provide a security blanket for the board.

3. If these alternatives are not acceptable and you do not feel that you want to assume the burden of a prudent man, then you should by all means resign. I hope you won't, because all banks need boards composed of men of high integrity, courage, wisdom, compassion, and varied experience.

CHARLES M. VAN HORN

What a Bank Supervisor Expects of a Director

OVER A CENTURY AGO the first Comptroller of the Currency recognized that the survival of the newly organized national banking system depended on responsible directors and management. Ever since 1864 each director of a national bank has been required to take an oath that "he will, so far as the duty devolves on him, diligently and honestly administer the affairs of such association, and will not knowingly violate, or willingly permit to be violated, any of the provisions" of the National Bank Act. The obvious purpose of that provision was to impose precise duties and responsibilities upon the directors.

Whether it involves protection against internal fraud, the lending function, the investment function, or any other activity of the bank, both statutory and common law have placed ultimate responsibility firmly and squarely on the bank's board of directors. Legally, they represent the top echelon of management. Authority may be delegated, but the ultimate responsibility for supervising the affairs of the bank cannot thereby be avoided. Each member of your board and each of your executive officers ought to read carefully the booklet *Duties and Liabilities of Directors of National Banks*, published by the Office of the Comptroller of the Currency.

The Director's Role

During the decade of the 60s, the director's duties and responsibilities accelerated at a pace unparalleled in American banking history. Consider the numerous major decisions in diverse areas that you are now called upon to make: branch expansion, mergers, holding company formation, the use of EDP equipment, credit cards, factoring, direct leasing, and other banking innovations created to serve evolving public needs. Meanwhile, competition among banks and with nonbanking financial institutions has become more intense. This competition is not limited to the supply and use of bank funds; it extends to the very heart of banking, personnel.

Bank directors must pay particular attention to the bank's salary structure. Nowadays, banks are competing as never before with one another and with other industries for executive skills. Salaries are one rough measure of the importance our economy attaches to a particular profession.

Financial rewards for bank officers must be commensurate with their responsibilities and competitive not only within the banking industry but with other fields of business. Directors would be well advised to inaugurate a continuing review of the salaries of the bank's officers.

Shareholders and depositors, as well as bank supervisors, look to the directors to provide sound administration of the affairs of the bank. Therefore, the most important responsibility of directors is the selection and appointment of well-qualified officers. Also incumbent upon the directors are the supervision of performance of executive officers and the replacement of those who fail to measure up to reasonable standards of executive ability and efficiency.

Another fundamental aspect of the director's role involves the adoption of sound policies, clearly defined in writing. Ordinarily, loans constitute the major portion of a bank's assets and the main source of earnings. Moreover, it is my considered opinion that 90 percent of serious banking problems manifest themselves in the loan portfolio. Thus, the formulation of sound lending policies warrants the director's most careful consideration.

Lending Policy

After giving due weight to such relevant factors as the deposit structure, the ability of the staff to service loans, and the legitimate credit needs of the community, the board should set forth a bank's lending policy, crystallized into a comprehensive written statement.

The formal statement should avoid the pitfalls of being too brief and too vague. At a minimum, the following nine points should be covered:

1. The maximum amount that lending officers may approve.
2. A suitable aggregate loan total.
3. The proportion of various types of loans: commercial loans, term

loans, real estate loans, consumer loans, and others in the portfolio.

4. The geographic area from which loans should ordinarily be generated.

5. The complete and reliable credit information to be required of borrowers.

6. The written acknowledgement of the borrower, at the inception of the loan, of his understanding of repayment arrangements.

7. The types of loans and collateral considered desirable for the bank's portfolio.

8. The types of loans and collateral considered inappropriate for the bank's portfolio.

9. The periodic review, inspection, and administration of loans after disbursement.

During the last few years our examination reports have revealed a sharp increase in the volume of loans subject to criticism. One of the principal contributing factors is the lack of effective loan administration. Many loans which were reasonably sound at their inception developed into problems and loan losses which might have been avoided if all banks, large and small, had reviewed each loan at the head office or a branch at least once each year, or more frequently if warranted by prevailing economic conditions.

Understand that the supervisory examiner does not review every single loan in the bank's portfolio. The size of line taken off for review by the examiner depends upon the size of the bank, management competency, adequacy of capital protection, and the asset condition as indicated by previous examination reports. The supervisory objective is to effect a thorough examination without wasting time on smaller loans of little or no significance in relation to the solvency of the bank. In delegating authority to the regional administrators to determine the size of line reviewed by national bank examiners, the Comptroller of the Currency has suggested the following guidelines:

In banks with total assets of less than $25 million, all lines of credit equal to or exceeding ¾ of one percent of gross capital funds are reviewed by the examiner. In this context, gross capital funds includes common and preferred stock, surplus, undivided profits, valuation reserves, capital notes, and debentures.

In banks with total assets of $25 million or more, it is suggested that the examiner review lines of credit exceeding ½ of one percent of gross capital funds.

For example, in a bank with $2 million in capital, the examiner might be looking at all loans in excess of $15,000. Generally, by reviewing loans of this size, plus the past due and smaller loans that we may have reasons for investigating, we cover approximately 80 percent of the dollar amount of the loan portfolio.

My purpose in calling your attention to the size of line reviewed by national bank examiners is to emphasize the necessity for management and directors to review periodically all loans, regardless of size.

The total line of each borrower, including installment and real estate loans as well as commercial loans, should be reviewed simultaneously.

Just as the board has the responsibility of formulating a lending policy, the directors must also establish and define by resolution an investment policy which fits the liquidity requirements of the bank. The investment policy statement should include:

1. Delegation of authority to buy and sell investments. The board should ratify all transactions made under delegated authority.

2. Distribution of maturities to reflect liquidity requirements and the trend of interest rates.

3. Investment quality standards.

4. Geographic origin of the obligations.

5. Limitation on obligations of one issuer, other than those of the U.S. Government.

6. Position in tax exempt issues.

Audit Procedures and Internal Controls

Every bank, regardless of size, should have an internal audit program which includes controls suited to its operations and designed to disclose irregularities and shortages. When the size of the bank warrants, a full-time auditor or auditing staff, responsible only to the board of directors, should be hired. The audit policy, formulated by the board of directors, should cover segregation and rotation of duties, mandatory vacations for officers and employees, dual control, selection and training of audit personnel, outside audits, direct verification, disbursement of loan proceeds, and a list of reports to be submitted at least monthly to the board of directors.

Examinations by the federal supervisory authorities do not purport to be audits and should not be relied on as such. As a general practice, such an examination does not include detailed checking of routine transactions or direct verification of individual loan and deposit balances. The importance of instituting effective audit procedures and internal controls cannot be overemphasized.

Formulation of lending, investment, and internal control policies must, of necessity, be the result of joint efforts of the executive management and the directors. Management should draft suitable recommendations for changes as circumstances warrant. No policy, however well conceived, should remain unchanged over the years.

Officers' Reports

It is not enough for the directors merely to set forth the policies in lending, investment, internal controls, and other areas. Continuous supervision must be exercised. The flow of significant information from management to the directors facilitates this testing of management performance against directors' standards and directives.

The lack of officers' reports to directors is one of the most serious deficiencies in present-day banking. In too many banks the active management doesn't want the directors to know what is going on in the bank. A bank officer whom I consider to be competent told me, "The biggest problem I have is my directors." Another bank officer admonished me, "Don't tell my directors about those assemblies; they're giving me too much trouble already." Bear in mind, however, that when serious problems come to our attention, the supervisory agency convenes the board of directors, not the active management, to obtain correction of the deficiencies.

The directors are responsible for implementation of their policies by honest, diligent, and competent officers and employees. Through reports of the discount committee, periodic officers' reports, or the directors' examination, the directors should know whether unsafe and unsound banking practices exist. You should not have to rely on the supervisory examiner for that.

In recent decades the principal underlying causes of serious banking problems have been management ineptness and self-dealing by management or directors.

Examiners are instructed to consider the recognition and effective handling of self-dealing as one of their most important functions. Among the common self-dealing practices are:

1. Loans to officers, directors, or large shareholders, or their interests, granted on an unsound basis or at preferential rates.

2. The use of correspondent accounts as compensating balances for loans to directors, officers, or large shareholders.

3. The payment of salaries or fees in excess of amounts warranted for the services performed.

4. The purchase and sale or lease rental of properties or other goods or services at prices unfavorable to the bank.

5. The use of the bank's funds for the payment of personal expenses of officers, directors, or large shareholders.

Frequently, our examinations reveal that self-dealing transactions are made without the awareness of the entire board of directors. A recommendation based upon this experience is that lending officers be required to report to the board any extension of credit by the bank, direct or indirect, to any director or officer, or to any partnership or corporation in which any director or officer may have a financial interest. Also, it is recommended that the entire board of directors take special action in connection with any transaction between the bank and one of its officers, directors, or large shareholders or their interests.

To avert the possibility of a conflict of interest or other breach of business morality, the board of directors of every bank should give serious consideration to the adoption of a code of ethics or a standard of conduct for the directors, officers, and employees of the bank. Directors and senior management would do well to remember Mark Twain's phrase: "Few things are harder to put up with than the annoyance of a good example."

Directors' Examination

From the inception of the National Banking System, the bylaws of national banks had it in view that the directors would make, or cause to be made, thorough periodic examinations to test the soundness of the bank's investments and loans, the effectiveness of management in implementing board policies, earnings and expenses, dividend policy, and the adequacy of insurance and fidelity coverage and the internal controls. Directors not qualified to perform the more technical aspects of the examination should employ a competent outside accountant to conduct the examination in their behalf. If that is done, the board or the examining committee should carefully review the account's report in order to comprehend fully the significance of the details of the report.

Supervisory Examination

Purpose and Scope

Such directors' examinations are of course in addition to the examinations made by the supervisory authority. The supervisory process provides a means of maintaining a constant vigil over the condition of the nation's banks. The supervisory examination has as its chief goals the determination of the bank's liquidity and solvency, present and prospective, and of the bank's compliance with the banking laws and regulations.

We are primarily concerned with the quality of the bank's assets, the sufficiency of internal controls, the adequacy of capital, and the soundness of management policies. The comptroller's office gives each bank a rating based upon information contained in the examination report.

Rating of Reports

Certain objective standards or rules of thumb serve as a foundation for our rating procedures. Upon this base the more subjective variables are weighed and balanced in arriving at a group or composite rating.

Capital adequacy, asset quality, and management are analyzed and rated in turn. In the end, an overall or composite rating is assigned.

Although the supervisory rating is not revealed to directors, an explanation of the major factors considered in rating a national bank might enable you to come up with a reasonable judgment of your own institution.

Capital Adequacy

Capital adequacy is appraised in relation to the character of the bank's management and its assets and deposit position as a going institution under normal conditions. We look for a reasonable margin of safety, with due regard to the bank's capacity to furnish the broadest service to the public.

Traditional capital-to-risk assets and capital-to-total-deposit ratios are no longer relied upon because of their arbitrary nature. In evaluating capital adequacy the comptroller's office has considered the following factors: the quality of management, the liquidity of assets, the history of earnings and the retention thereof, the quality and character of ownership, the burden of meeting occupancy expenses, the potential volatility of the bank's deposit structure, the quality of operating procedures, and the bank's capacity to meet present and future financial needs of its trade area, considering the competition it faces.

In addition, we use a formula which relates capital to the volume of loans and discounts. The numerator is the total of gross loans and discounts. Total capital accounts including reserves constitute the denominator. This loans-times-capital ratio is a first, quick test of capital adequacy. Where gross loans exceed seven times the total capital accounts, the bank is scrutinized closely. We analyze the loan portfolio for quality and liquidity. Commercial paper, brokers' loans, municipal loans, and loans guaranteed or insured by the U.S. government are among those taken into consideration. Application of any rule of thumb obviously requires judgment. By carefully evaluating all relevant factors, the comptroller's office avoids penalizing well-managed, profit-conscious banks.

Asset Quality

A bank's asset quality is measured initially by relating the aggregate volume of assets classified substandard, doubtful, or loss to gross capital funds, including reserves. Each bank is assigned to one of four categories.

Generally speaking, banks with total classified assets of less than 20 percent of gross capital funds receive an "A" rating. Banking, after all, is a risk business and the evaluation of credit involves matters of judgment. It is certainly no reflection upon management or the directors if an examiner criticizes a moderate volume of the bank's assets.

When classified assets amount to more than 20 percent but less than 40 percent of gross capital funds, the bank earns a "B" rating.

A "C" rating goes to banks with classified assets aggregating more than 40 percent but less than 80 percent of gross capital funds, and a "D" rating to banks with classified assets in excess of 80 percent of gross capital funds. With few exceptions, a bank in the "C" or "D" category, with classified assets equal to 40 percent or more of the capital structure, requires more than a normal degree of supervisory attention.

In connection with the examination of "C" and "D" rated banks, a national bank examiner usually convenes the board of directors to appraise them of the situation and to obtain assurances that corrective measures will be instituted. Incidentally, examiner's meetings with directors are not limited to those situations. National bank examiners are always pleased to meet with directors or the executive committee upon request at the conclusion of the examination. Such meetings give the directors and officers of national banks the benefit of seeing their bank through the examiner's eyes.

Earnings are extremely important from a supervisory standpoint. A good earning bank is a more viable competitor and, normally, a more progressive institution overall.

We compare the individual bank with banks of similar size. The FDIC now makes this useful information quickly available to all insured banks. Make sure to review the copy of the FDIC summary mailed to your bank. You can thus readily compare your bank's performance with the earnings of institutions in your size group.

If your bank's earnings are less than average for banks of similar size, the board or a committee thereof should carefully analyze the causes of your unfavorable situation and consider the steps necessary to bring about improvements.

Management

Only after weighing capital adequacy and asset quality is management assigned a rating. Clearly, it would be difficult to assign the highest management rating, "strong," in a bank which had a heavy volume of classified assets, inadequate controls and safeguards, violations of law, or inadequate capital protection. Conversely, it would not be consistent to give management a rating of "poor," the lowest rating, in a bank free of asset, operating, or capital problems.

In judging the quality of management, we take into consideration the overall condition of the bank: its liquidity position, its earnings compared with banks of similar size, the adequacy of its credit files, the effectiveness of collection efforts, the quality and distribution of the investment account, the adequacy of internal controls, the efficiency of operations, the provision made for management succession, and the bank's service to the community.

Composite or Group Rating

A group or composite rating, based largely upon the combination which results from the earlier evaluation of capital, asset quality, and management, is assigned to each examination report.

Group #1 banks are sound in every respect. Fortunately for supervisors, most banks fall into this category.

Group #2 banks have one or more unfavorable factors, such as asset weaknesses ranging from moderate to moderately heavy, inadequate capital, or less than satisfactory management. This rating would also apply when certain special factors prevail, such as lack of adequate supervision by the directors, detrimental domination by one or more persons, significant deficiencies in auditing or internal controls, or unfavorable effects resulting from local economic conditions.

Group #3 banks are characterized by an excessive volume of asset problems in relation to capital, serious management deficiencies, exposure to extremely adverse local economic conditions, or a combination of these or other problems which could reasonably develop into a situation urgently requiring emergency aid from shareholders.

Group #4 banks are confronted with asset problems of an extremely serious nature and with gross inadequacy of management and directorate so that shareholder aid is urgently required. If such aid is not forthcoming, drastic supervisory measures appear to be warranted.

The Director's Responsibility

A copy of the supervisory examination report is addressed to the board of directors. Each director should insist on reviewing the report page by page and item by item. On page two of the report, you may find listed violations of law, inadequate credit information, internal operating deficiencies, policy weaknesses, or other matters requiring attention. Once put on notice, through the supervisory examination report or otherwise, that deficiencies exist, the director has the duty of instituting improvements. The steps taken or contemplated to alleviate the supervisory criticism should be recorded in the minutes of the board meeting, because the courts have held that disregard of the direction of the officers appointed by law to examine the affairs of the bank is a violation of law.

The bank's officers may not be subject to the same statutory and common law liabilities as the directors; nevertheless, they have a moral obligation to keep the directors fully informed if the bank is to function at maximum efficiency. In today's banking environment, the coordination of efforts of bank directors and officers is vital. the officers should constantly endeavor to encourage maximum participation by each director.

The directorate should function somewhat like a football coach who knows all of the rules and sets up the game plan, but leaves execution thereof to the team. By attending board and committee meetings, by asking questions, by reviewing meaningful officers' reports on the bank's activities, by participating in the directors' examination, and by carefully reviewing supervisory examination reports, the bank director can become better informed in the best interests of the shareholders, the depositors, and the welfare of the bank's service area.

An analysis by the FDIC of bank failures over the last twelve years revealed that lack of diligence of directors was a contributing factor:

> In general, directors of the closed banks abandoned their vital duties and functioned as "rubber stamp bodies" for the controlling parties of the banks. We have examples of directors failing to establish clear overall policies, failing to review all loans that were made along with supporting collateral and papers, failing to review all cash items and overdrafts at periodic intervals, failing to use reasonable efforts to collect slow assets, failing to control expenditures properly, failing to establish internal routines and controls, failing to conduct the required examinations and failing to maintain adequate primary and excess fidelity bond coverage. In some cases, where sound procedures were provided for, the directors failed to follow-up their directives to see that all were being carried out. In some embezzlement cases, opportunity was offered to the defaulting officers or employees through the failure of bank management to provide simple safeguards, such as requiring all officers and employees to take annual vacations.

Summary and Conclusion

Now to summarize. As a minimum, the supervisor expects the bank director to do the following things:

1. Provide for competent, resourceful executive officers, including successor management.
2. Formulate clearly defined policies covering lending, investments, internal controls, and other activities of the bank.
3. Effectively supervise implementation of board policies.
4. Know the strengths and limitations of the bank's active management.
5. Attend regular and special board meetings and committee meetings, and participate actively in their deliberations.
6. Insure the keeping of accurate and complete minutes of all meetings.
7. Carefully review written reports submitted by various committees of directors.

8. Require and carefully review periodic management reports.

9. Carefully examine the affairs of the bank or cause same to be done on your behalf by a competent, outside, independent accountant.

10. Carefully review, in detail, reports of examinations submitted by supervisory authorities and outside, independent accountants.

11. Take prompt, vigorous steps to eliminate weaknesses cited in supervisory reports.

12. Know the banking needs of the bank's service area and render the bank responsive to those needs.

13. Be familiar with banking laws and regulations, asset values, financial statements, capital adequacy, liquidity, and related matters dealing with policy formulation.

14. Maintain an unblemished personal and business reputation.

15. Refrain from self-dealing transactions and police your associates on the board.

16. Keep inviolate all confidential information relating to affairs of those who deal with the bank.

In the election of directors, shareholders confer an honor which carries with it clearly defined common law liabilities as well as statutory responsibilities. The shareholders have every right to expect that the directors will ascertain the nature of their obligations and discharge them accordingly. As banks broaden the scope of their facilities and services, the director's task becomes even more complicated. New issues are constantly calling for the exercise of sound judgment. Upon the wisdom of your decisions rests much of the vigor and strength of our commercial banking system. Supervisors are well aware that yours is truly a position of great prestige and important responsibilities.

PART TWO

Management Policies and Procedures

JAMES E. SMITH

Changes Going on in Banking

I WANTED YOU TO KNOW how we, in fulfilling the regulatory function, value the contributions made by diligent and knowledgeable directors. When you do your work well, that of assuring that your bank is conducting its business—the business of credit extension and investment of depositors' money—in a manner which progressively advances your community and assures and maintains the soundness and stability of your banking institution, you make our job, the job of the regulator, far, far easier. You greatly lessen our burdens.

The topic that was assigned to me for this discussion is "Changes Going On in Banking." Some, perhaps most of what I shall be discussing, may not seem to be directly responsive to that title, for I should like to consider principally some of the changes and some of the things that are going on in the office of the Comptroller of the Currency.

For those who do not have the wondrous pleasure and privilege of being part of the national banking system, I shall say that it is the responsibility of the Comptroller of the Currency to charter, regulate, and supervise the national banks of this country. We have over 4,600 banks, with assets in excess of 450 billion dollars, some 60 to 65 percent of the total assets in the commercial banking system.

We do have some things which I think are important under way in the office. While they may not necessarily effect changes in the banking business, some of them will; all of them are, at least, reflective of changes that are occurring in this great industry.

I think the most exciting project that we have under way at present, and one that is just getting off the ground, is the undertaking of a very comprehensive and broad-based evaluation of our mission as the regulators of the national banking system, with primary attention given to the traditional backbone of all of our functions, the examination process.

You might ask why we are doing this. The present Comptroller is of the opinion that every organization, public and private, ought to take a self-critical look at itself periodically to see how it is in fact performing its mission.

This office was established in 1863 by President Lincoln, and in the time that has elapsed since then we have not undertaken such a comprehensive evaluation. It did seem to me that it was timely, after more than a century, to see how we were doing our job.

Secondly, and really more importantly, as all of you who have been associated with the great business of commercial banking know, the last ten years, most especially, have produced the most dramatic of changes in the way this business is done. We have seen remarkable growth in the services that banks and holding companies are providing in the financial field to American business and the American public. We have seen incredible changes in the structure of liabilities and deposits of commercial banks, and what interactive effects these changes have on the asset side of the institution.

So we are now in a period where considerable change has already occurred. I think we are in for a great deal more change, and if I read the tea leaves right, the next ten years are going to produce changes that are at least as dramatic as those which occurred in the first ten years.

We, in fulfilling the regulatory function, have a very considerable obligation and responsibility to make certain that we are keeping abreast of what the industry is doing—that we are undertaking our regulatory mission in a way that not only assures the safety and soundness of these institutions, but facilitates their ability to do their job in the highly competitive financial world of today.

So I view our study partly as a propitious occasion to play a little catchup ball, because I think that perhaps we have not entirely kept pace with the industry in the last ten years. But far more importantly, I see the fruits of this study as positioning us to move with the industry and to do our job for the benefit of the public and of the industry in a more modern and responsive way over the rest of this century.

What kinds of things do we hope to find and to achieve by such a study? I might give you a little background on the study technique itself.

We had at one point considered doing the job in house, but we rejected that idea, principally for two reasons. First, to do such a massive job in house would require us to take many, if not all, of our very best and most senior people off the line. And that would not be at all helpful in the current performance of our mission.

Secondly, to do this kind of comprehensive self-criticism, and to do it in house, would still leave questions as to the credibility of the results. So we have gone outide; we put out a very detailed proposal, or request for proposals. We now have in hand ten fully responsive proposals from major accounting firms and major management consulting firms. Some were so overwhelmed by the size of the request that we find some of the big eight accounting firms joining with some of the major management consulting firms to give us a joint venture proposal.

In the majority of the proposals that we have in hand, prominent banking lawyers, prominent banking professors, and prominent banking consultants have been included. I think this is very important and very hopeful. They are the group that I would describe as the conceptualists. These are the people who, it is to be hoped, have some sense of where this industry is going to be moving in the next two decades. And any evaluation of our work must proceed from that sort of conceptual foundation, and I feel that we have in these proposals the prospect of some very effective study projects.

What would we like to achieve? I can give you three examples of what we are interested in. Number one involves our own personnel. I have now pretty well traveled the length and breadth of this country in the eight or nine months that I have been in office. I've met literally dozens of our examiners in the field, and almost all of our regional administrators on location. (I have met all of them in Washington.) We have a remarkably talented and dedicated group of people.

My concern is that we have those people properly deployed and employed. And more importantly, for those who are entering our organization, I'm greatly concerned as to how effectively we are serving them, in terms of their training and professional development. This is no simple task for an organization such as ours. We have something over two thousand people in the field deployed in fourteen regional locations and in many, many more subregional locations.

To try to develop an educational and professional development program for an organization that is so broadly dispersed geographically is not an easy task. We're working at it. I think we can do a better job of it, and we hope that will be one of the fruits of this study and evaluation.

The second example—and this is one that touches my particular fancy—has to do with computerized systems analysis. I am not a systems man. I'm awed by what I see systems people doing, and what things are possible with the developing technology of computers and other types of automatic machines; but we in the comptroller's office are running a bit behind in this area. We ourselves are not computerized. We are moving very rapidly, however, to fill that void.

But I think that in the whole field of bank regulation and bank supervision we have just begun to scratch the surface of what we can do with the available benefits of a computerized industry—and certainly the banking industry itself is one of the most highly computerized industries in this country.

I think that once we have our systems in place, not only in Washington but in the regions, we can begin to think of links with the banks, which will permit our people in the field to perform some of the more rote and mechanical functions of the examination by machine, much more quickly and painlessly than they do it today. This would free much more of their time to be devoted to the analytical business of examining a bank, of evaluations of credits, of evaluations of how the bank is organized—what its policies are, and whether those policies as stated are in fact being implemented and effected in the operation of the bank.

Out of this, I see the role of the bank examiner becoming what one prominent banking consultant has predicted for a time perhaps ten years in the future, that of a management consultant with clout.

Last among my examples is one that I hope can produce some real benefits for the industry, in terms of more enlightened, more flexible, less dogmatic regulation. I'm still convinced, given the genius of man, that we can develop some real analytical tools, some objective standards and tests for making some reliable qualitative judgments about banking management in general, and how a particular bank is in fact being managed.

And I think if we can develop those tools, those standards, those methods of analysis, then a whole new world of flexibility will open up in the area of bank regulation. One item that immediately comes to mind, one that warms the cockles of all bankers' hearts, is the lessening of dogmatic rules with respect to capital.

We talk frequently in the comptroller's office about how we are less dogmatic than others, and how we make our judgments with respect to bank capital, not on certain traditional ratios, but on a variety of considerations, one of the most prominent being the quality of bank management. I would be less than honest with you if I told you that I think we, today, have the tools in place to make the kind of objective evaluations of bank management that we should, with respect to such important questions as capital.

I see the development of these tools as a product of this study. These are but a few of the objectives. We figure the study will take some fifteen months. It's going to cost us, and it's going to cost you, the national banks, a piece of change in the process. But I think it's going to be worthwhile, and I am mighty hopeful that it is going to produce results that will permit us to do a more constructive job, thereby permitting you to do a more progressive and effective job in your own banking climate.

We are also doing some things in the area of intensified regulation. I do hope that we learned some important things from our unhappy experience with the United States National Bank in San Diego, which involved the largest bank failure in the history of commercial banking. I think that perhaps we were lacking in the highest order of sensitivity to certain types of practices. We have taken one regulatory step already, which certainly derives from the United States National Bank experience. That is the application of new regulations, which have been issued by all of the federal banking agencies, the Fed, the FDIC, and the Comptroller, with respect to the so-called standby letter of credit arrangement.

For the first time we are proposing (we're still in the comment period) that single borrower lending limits be applied to the standby letter of credit arrangements. Also, the limitations on both size of commitment and the requirements for collateral, with respect to loans to affiliates, will also be applicable to this particular credit facility.

We will also be requiring, for the first time, that banks indicate in a footnote to their balance sheets the aggregate of these contingent liabilities, so that those doing business with the bank, those who are interested in purchasing either the equity or the debt securities of the bank, will have some understanding of the potential liabilities that a particular institution has.

In the case of the United States National Bank, these arrangements were used most imprudently. Irresponsibly, I think, is probably a more accurate word. There was some view at the federal level that we should just ban the use of standby letters of credit. Thank goodness that view did not prevail. It is a useful credit facility for a commercial bank to have available, and most especially for those commercial banks, that find themselves from day to day in head-to-head competition with major international financial institutions.

But far and away the most serious problem present at the United States National Bank, and this is one that ought to be of particular interest to you as bank directors, was the fact that this was a case of self-dealing lending having run riot—the most egregious case in the history of the banking industry.

When I speak of self-dealing lending, I'm speaking of a bank lending to the business affiliates of officers and directors of that bank. It is not *per se* unlawful. I do not think that is generally understood by the public, but for the safety and the soundness of the institution, indeed for the self-esteem of this industry, and for the maintenance of its credibility with the public, self-dealing lending must not occur on any standards other than the highest standards of both credit extension and credit administration. That means full compliance with applicable law and regulation, and full compliance with the very best practices of credit administration, in terms of documentation and of follow-up with loans once they are made.

Now, we are going to take a new heightened interest in this variety of loan. And this is not a threat; this is a statement of fact. The banks examined by the Comptroller of the Currency which have such loans that are not up to snuff, when it comes to compliance with law and regulation in terms of credit administration, may expect those loans to be criticized.

In the very near future we are intending to take one regulatory step to facilitate our ability to track this kind of lending. We will be issuing a regulation which will require that every national bank maintain at its head office, and in a current form, updated monthly if necessary, forms which we will provide the bank. This will be a standard form. It will be subject to the terms of the criminal statutes, which will require each executive officer and each director of every national bank to keep currently on file a list of his business affiliations. And the definition of business affiliate will be rather broadly drawn.

These will not be reports filed with us. They will be reports maintained in a confidential fashion at the head office of the bank; but they will be available to our examiners when they enter the bank. This will permit them to move immediately to the note case and to make certain that any loans to such business affiliates are in full compliance with law and regulation.

Most of you are not in the day-to-day management and operation of your banks. You are outside directors. You are engaged in other businesses. And so you would not necessarily know that this industry has grown up in a period and under circumstances where, by reason of the tragedies and travails of the 1930s, it finds itself (in my personal view) operating under some very considerable constraints upon effective competition.

Among those constraints are certain structural rigidities that occur in state law, with respect to branching, multioffice opportunities, home office protection, etc. At the federal level the time and savings deposit rates of commercial banks, and more recently of thrift institutions, savings and loan associations, and mutual savings banks, are subject to regulation and control by three federal financial agencies: the Federal Reserve Board, the FDIC, of which I am also a director, and the Federal Home Loan Bank Board.

I find it very difficult to speak about, or to characterize, the maximum regulation of interest rates which banks and other deposit financial institutions may pay on time and savings deposits—*consumer* time and savings deposits. I find it very difficult to characterize that in any other way than as governmental price fixing.

All of you who are in other lines of business have been recently exposed, over the last couple of years, to government regulation of prices and wages. You know how stultifying and how destructive that can be for innovative and competitively-inclined management.

The banking industry has lived with this around its neck for some forty years now. The First National City Bank of New York has recently released a monograph on *Competition in the Financial Field.* If none of you have had the chance to read it, I strongly urge you to do so. And don't kid yourselves for a moment that the only competition that is out there now, or that is going to be out there over the balance of this century, is reflected in the Savings and Loan Association that happens to be across the street.

Look down the street at the branch offices of Sears, or Montgomery Ward, or GMAC, or Ford Motor Credit, or GE Credit. This monograph points out that in terms of consumer installment receivables Sears Roebuck tops the top three commercial banks in this country. They are not operating with any of these aforementioned limitations on rate.

Now we're only talking about the asset side of the ledger. The day is not far off when the same network that is available for this extension of consumer credit will also get into the consumer savings market. I think the day is not far off when the Searses, and the GEs, and the GMACs are going to be out in the local market with consumer savings certificates of some type, and that is going to be directly competitive with the deposit-raising abilities of commercial banks and thrift institutions. That's when the pinch is really going to come, if your industry continues to operate under the harness of the ceiling-rate regulation enunciated in Washington, D.C.

The rationale of this was that in the 1930s some concluded that the problems of financial institutions at that time occurred because of cutthroat competition as to interest rates.

I'm not going to argue with you as to whether or not that is myth; but we are living in a quite different climate today than we were forty years ago, in terms of the safeguards and checks and balances that are in place in the form of federal regulation. I am convinced that we, as regulators, can deal with those individual cases of people who step strongly beyond the speed limit in this area.

Certainly, we ought to be able to develop screening techniques to track liability costs, and to determine whether a particular institution is vastly out of line with others, and therefore likely to get into trouble on the asset side of the ledger trying to cover its liability costs. It's my opinion that we ought not to continue to regulate this great industry on the basis of what we conclude is the lowest common denominator of managerial talent or prudence. The banking industry has too great a mission to perform for the American public and for American business to be operated under that type of governmental regulation.

I think these changes in the world of finance are going to occur. I would urge you, as members of the banking industry, to get out ahead of them, to take the initiative in seeing to it that the banking industry is part of these changes rather than the victim of them.

JOHN A. CADDELL

Outside Directors' Functions

I WOULD LIKE to pose some questions, suggest some answers and give you some suggestions as to the function of an outside director. I do not claim to be an expert on the subject, although in preparing this presentation I have read a number of articles on the subject and have talked to several people, including bank officers, outside directors, and people with no official bank connections. I think our best chance of learning something helpful on this subject will be to draw on our own experience.

My first question to you comes from the title of this article: *What are the functions of an outside director?* Before answering this question we need to answer a second question: *Why serve as an outside director?* To find the answer to this question we must first define the function, purpose, and objective of a bank. In other words: *Why operate a bank?*

The answers to these questions involve the entire purpose of the assemblies for bank directors which are sponsored by the Foundation of the Southwestern Graduate School of Banking at SMU. And the purpose of these assemblies is to: (1) increase *your* understanding of how *you* can serve *your* bank; (2) indicate the ways in which *you* can best serve as a representative of *your* bank in *your* community; (3) provide for *you* a better understanding of and respect for the functions of *your* bank's management; and (4) acquaint *you* more fully with issues of critical interest to *your* bank in particular and to banking in general. In considering the questions I have posed, the first question we should dispose of is:

"*Why operate a bank?*"

The late Chester Rude, in his discussion of "Sound Credit Administration and the Director" in 1968, made the statement that the function of commercial banking is: (1) to act as a reservoir of surplus funds of the community, and (2) to lend these funds to those in the community who need them. I agree with this definition wholeheartedly. According to this theory, the primary justification for the existence of a bank is public service; profit for stockholders is only secondary.

Others will disagree. Charles Agemain has said that the purpose of operating a bank is to make money for the stockholders and that the only thing that matters is net earnings per share after taxes. I admit that I attach some importance to this feature of the operation and that I would like what little bank stock I own to increase in value, but I feel that the first and foremost mission of a bank is public service; a bank is an agency by which the people of a given community can make a cooperative effort to improve their community.

There are definitely two schools of thought on the question of the primary reason for operating a bank, and nearly every board of directors will have people with differing views on the subject. Among the other directors of my own bank is the president of the bank, and even though I try to be highly altruistic, I feel that he, as chief executive officer of the bank, should be sharply attuned to profitable operation as his guiding star. Another of our directors is a grandson of the founder of our bank and is a third-generation director, following his father and grandfather. The other one is a prominent and highly successful businessman and a large landowner. Both of them are probably more inclined than I am toward emphasizing the importance of the profit motive. Even I have mixed emotions. I think we will all agree that the very first responsibility of a bank is to its depositors. But there will be some slight disagreement as to whether the stockholder or the community comes second.

This prompts us to the question: *Why serve as an outside director?* or *Why, indeed, do I serve as a bank director?* (The fact is that the dangers are great, and the growing tendency of minority stockholders to file suits against banks and their directors makes it quite hazardous to serve.) I would say that the primary justification for serving as an outside director is to fulfill a public service obligation; it is one way for him to pay a part of his civic rent.

One reason a man accepts an invitation to serve as a bank director is that in most cases he feels flattered by such an invitation; he is influenced to some extent by the honor and the prestige that he feels go with the position.

The profit motive is another reason for serving as an outside director. There are those who own enough percentage interest in a given bank to make it worth their while to serve on the board of directors to promote their personal financial interests in the bank. This is rare, however, and most directors, particularly in the small-town banks with which I am familiar, do not own enough stock in the banks in which they are directors to justify the time and effort that they should expend to do their jobs properly. I thoroughly enjoy receiving my director's fees, and I look with much interest on the fine increase we have had in the market value of our bank's stock; but I certainly could not afford to give all the time, energy, and effort I do to the bank for the financial gain I receive in director's fees, dividends, and possible enhancement in value of my stock. I am sure that many will disagree with me, but my answer to the question *Why serve as an outside director?* is that the only real justification is to serve our community.

As we consider the motivation for a person to accept election to the board of directors of a bank, it is also interesting to review the reasons a bank has for selecting an outside director. The consensus of the opinions that I have sampled in articles I have read and in talks I have had with bankers on this subject is that a bank selects an outside director for the following reasons (which are not necessarily mentioned in the order of their importance): (1) to take advantage of his standing in the community, (2) to get his personal business, (3) to get business he can influence, (4) to use his depth of knowledge and his experience in his own line of endeavor, and (5) to make use of the soundness of his judgment and such advice as he can give with a minimum amount of preparation.

This brings us then to the final question: *What are the functions of an outside director?* My general answer would be: (1) to furnish a safe, secure, well-run, successful depository to take care of the surplus funds of the community; and (2) to lend these funds wisely, treating them always as trust funds, but using them in such a way as to help develop the community.

In accomplishing these broad objectives the outside director should leave to the officers of the bank all routine operating decisions, but should use his best efforts and wisest judgment in giving direction in policy matters and in promoting the best interests of the bank with the depositors and borrowers.

In providing for the safety of the deposits, as well as the investment of the stockholders, the directors can promote their own interests and protect themselves against possible liability by *requiring* the bank to have written policies on a great many different matters. The most important items are: (1) the loan policy, (2) the investment policy, and (3) the internal control policy. This list can be extended to: (4) trust business, (5) conflicts of interest, (6) the purchase and sale of the bank's own stock by directors, (7) the release of information, (8) contributions and memberships of the bank, and (9) a variety of other matters.

There is a reluctance to have policies written down, but the efficiency of the bank and safety of the deposits and the safety of the officers and directors can be greatly enhanced by having as many of these matters as possible reduced to writing, particularly the important first three—a written *loan policy*, a written *investment policy*, and a written *internal control policy*.

To contribute to the success of a bank, a director must be a member of the team and an enthusiastic supporter of his own bank. His first step is to bring in his own account and that of his business.

A director should beat the bushes for new business. Every year his bank will lose 10 to 15 percent of its accounts as customers move away, go out of business, die, or just plain get mad. Just to stay in the same place a bank must be finding one new customer each year for every eight old customers it has. An outside director is in better position to help the bank get new business than are the officers and employees themselves. Most of them don't seem to realize this and don't work at it as much as they should. I do not say that an outside director should neglect his own personal business to act as a bank salesman, but he should be ever watchful for new banking business in his normal contacts and a continuous booster of his bank among business and social acquaintances.

All bank directors have the obligation to maintain the complete secrecy of all that takes place in the bank. An outside director should exercise extraordinary caution in this regard.

A director's obligation to the community is that he maintain a strong bank. Again this can be accomplished by wise loan, investment, and internal control policies which are in writing and carefully followed. The failure of a privately owned business hurts a community, but not nearly so much as the failure of a bank. The bank's money should be loaned intelligently and in such a way as best to promote the welfare and development of the community, and in such a way as to get the money back.

Among the important responsibilities of outside directors are: (1) to attend meetings of the board regularly, (2) to require examinations and audits, and (3) to try to learn something about the banking business.

An outside director should act as a messenger of good will for his bank in the community. He should conduct himself in his public and private affairs in such a manner as to be a symbol of the bank, inspiring the confidence of the public and enhancing the public image of the bank.

The final function, responsibility, and duty of an outside director is to get off the board when he is no longer able to do the things I have talked about, for reason—age, health, place of residence, demands of his own business, travel, or any other reason.

To recapitulate, the following list of things I think an outside director should do is compiled from my own experience and my own ideas and from suggestions I have read and have had from other interested people. I am sure that I have not covered everything and that no one will agree with all of the items I would include.

1. An outside director should give the bank his own business.

2. He should be a walking, talking salesman for the bank, helping to bring in all the new business he possibly can.

3. He should help advertise the bank, be a messenger of good will for the bank, and work constantly to enhance the public image of the bank.

4. He should maintain complete secrecy as to the business of the customers of the bank.

5. He should be regular in attendance at the meetings of the board.

6. He should require examinations and audits and carefully review all such reports.

7. He should learn enough about the banking business to establish intelligently general policies for the bank and to see that those policies are carried out by the officers.

8. He should not interfere with routine operating decisions, but should leave these to the officers and employees of the bank.

9. He should require written policies on all important matters, at least on the loan policy, the investment policy, and the internal control policy.

10. He should avoid self-dealing and conflicts of interest.

11. He should never be a "rubber stamp" for the use of the bank's officers.

12. He should insure that the bank has a beneficial influence on the economy of its community.

13. He should get off the board when he has outlived his usefulness.

GORDON G. WITTENBERG

An Outside Director Looks at His Functions

I AM AN ARCHITECT in Little Rock, Arkansas. I'm not a banker, but I *am* a bank director, and I am interested in my job. I believe I have accepted the responsibility with my eyes wide open, and, while I consider it a great honor to serve on the board of my bank as a comparatively young man, I recognize the responsibilities—and the opportunities—that I have assumed.

Our Bank, First National in Little Rock, is not owned by one individual, one family, or even a majority group. Our stock ownership is widespread and not under anybody's control. We meet, we vote, and we act without the fear or the frustration of the knowledge that anything and everything we do is subject to the possible overriding vote of some individual or group. And I think it is important for every member of our board to *know* that his or her (incidentally, we are the first bank in our community to place a woman, Dr. Bessie Moore, on our Board) vote *counts* and is not simply an expression of feeling that someone else may accept or reject because of majority ownership. I'm not against majority ownership, but I think it is important to understand.

Now they tell me that all banks are different. I can accept that, just as I can accept the fact that all building plans designed by my office are different. On the other hand, I know that there are certain basic similarities between one building and the next. I believe this applies to banking as well.

Let's look briefly at why banks are in business, which I think we sometimes tend to forget. I know our bank does. Directors must occasionally remind management of why we are in business, and the reverse is certainly true also.

Clearly, our primary job is to be one of the depositories of the money in our community—the operating funds and surplus funds of companies and individuals—to safeguard it, to serve as a conduit of commerce for interchange of these funds between businesses and individuals, and to transfer funds on the order of our customers. As a corollary, our job is to lend the funds—or *rent* them—to businesses and individuals in our community who need the money for short periods, and who will pay rent on the money when they return the principal on a specified date. But beyond those primary functions we have certain other reasons for being in business. Let's see if we can agree that we have the following responsibilities as a corporation doing business in our community:

1. The responsibility to our *depositors* and our *customers*, as I have already stated.

2. A responsibility to our *shareholders* to earn a fair return on their invested capital.

3. A responsibility to our *community*.

4. A responsibility to our *employees*, without whose common aims and goals our bank could never be so successful.

5. And, certainly, a responsibility to the many other segments of the public in our community.

Let's look quickly at the Policy Guidelines of the Comptroller of the Currency:

> Directors have been placed in positions of trust by the shareholders of the bank. Both statutory and common law have placed responsibility for the management of banks . . . (whether it involves the lending or investing function) . . . (protection against internal fraud) . . . or any other activity of the bank, firmly and squarely on the members of the bank's Board of Directors. The directors of a national bank may delegate the day to day routine of conducting the bank's business but they cannot delegate to their officers and employees the responsibility for the consequences resulting from unsound or imprudent policies and practices.

I believe the FDIC and state authorities have about the same interpretation so far as state chartered banks are concerned. Now, how do we go about this?

I subscribe to the theory that the leadership of my bank—the top executive officers and the executive committee of the board—should be constantly alert to find people in the community who might be considered to fill vacancies on our board of directors as they occur—people who will accept the responsibilities we have just discussed. I believe a good board of directors should have reasonably full representation from the different areas of business, agriculture, the professions, and education. And the consumer should be represented too. Incidentally, we have a fine young newspaper editor on our board who really guards consumer interests. I'm not saying you ought to go out and get a consumer activist from one of the consumer agencies to serve on your board; but it would be well for you, like us, to have a director who remembers the consumer when money gets tight.

I expect a board of directors to be more than just the cronies or close friends of the president or chairman. I want different viewpoints on the board of directors. I like to have a fellow who can grill an executive officer and make him feel uncomfortable if he isn't up to date on his responsibilities. Somehow, he makes me feel more comfortable, because I know he's there with that sharp, quick, probing mind. Sometimes this director may be a little too quick . . . but, like the cross-eyed discus thrower at the county track meet, while he may not break many records, he sure keeps the crowd alert.

A board of directors must be involved. I've heard one of the most experienced bankers in America, Charlie Agemain, who knows more about banking than I would learn if I lived to be a hundred years old, speak against *committees*; *but* he is an *inside* director, and a good one, *not* an outside director, seeking a way to be sure that he fulfills his total responsibilities when he's on the job just a small part of the time.

I want board of director involvement; not in management, but in determining policy in each major function for which the board must accept responsibility. And I want regular review of bank operations to see if that policy is being carried out and to review and update the policy as changes occur. And I want to remember that it has been said, "If we're doing anything the way it was done five years ago in our bank, we're ten years behind the times."

I want a group of working board committees. Certainly, by law, we must have an audit or examining committee, a trust committee (if we have a trust department), and a directors' loan committee, unless the board as a whole acts as the loan committee.

Beyond that, I want an officer personnel committee, not just to listen to the president recommend promotions and raises and to pass them on rubber-stamped to the board of directors; but to make certain, for instance, that by annual or semiannual review with executive officers, provision for management succession as a prime executive responsibility is being accomplished all along the line, not just at the top. I want an opportunity for a few well-chosen directors to become better acquainted with the young men in our bank on the way up, and this is one way to do it.

And I want an insurance committee to study in detail the insurance and fidelity bond coverage of our bank, not just with the officers of the bank, but with the industry representatives who may recommend a better or more thorough way. While most of us are vigilant in supervising loans, I believe that, likewise, most of us are negligent in reviewing bank investments; so I want a bank investments committee that periodically reviews the investment portfolio for changes that should be made.

I want a capital structure committee to study, at least once a year, the long-range capital needs which our bank is likely to have, and to report those needs to the board with policy recommendations as it sees fit. There may also be need for small board committees to consider stock options and to administer the retirement policies of the bank.

I expect the board committees of my bank to help management develop written policies for every major department of the bank. And I want brief but regular reports by the director/chairman of these committees. I expect management to design reports that are readable, understandable, comparable, and meaningful in helping the director/chairman in reporting on execution of bank policies.

Some banks have one or more directors who are careless about attending meetings. I expect to attend meetings of the board of my bank the greater part of the time, and to be absent only when compelling business prohibits my attendance. I expect other directors to do the same. A director who does not regularly attend meetings is denying his bank the service of someone else who could contribute more, work harder, and better meet the needs of this very complex process.

Banks have been notoriously slow in providing for retirement of board members, although they have done a fairly good job of providing for retirement of bank personnel. A directors' retirement plan should be a part of the bank's by-laws. It should be carefully devised by a committee of the board of directors and thoroughly discussed by the board prior to approval. I understand that most banks now have adopted plans which would require directors to retire either on disability or no later than at seventy years of age, and some require retirement at sixty-five. This is a tough decision in a smaller bank with few directors, but it is a decision that our responsibilities require us to accept.

I owe my bank something, and I know it.

1. I owe the bank the courtesy of giving the bank all of my own business, or the major part of it if I am in a firm requiring several accounts. It must be known as "my bank."

2. The bank should expect me to work for new business for the bank, and to be alert to new customers who may be prospects for the bank.

3. I owe the bank the good judgment *not ever* to carry confidential bank business or discussion of a customer or a prospect's business outside the board room. It has been done—*and you know it has.* To do so is a flagrant breach of trust.

4. I owe my bank my attendance and participation in regular meetings, setting aside enough time to stay for the whole meeting, and I am also obligated to attend special meetings if called.

5. The bank has a right to expect me to conduct my own business and my personal life so as not to reflect against the good image of my bank, and the bank should expect me to resign from the board should my situation get in such bad shape that it might embarrass the bank.

6. I should know better than to ask for special rates, questionable loans, favors, and such; and I should know better than ever to exercise the strength of my position as a director to intimidate or take advantage of an officer or any of the personnel of my bank.

7. The executive officers of my bank have a right to expect me to stay out of management but to stay involved in policy, and to learn the difference between the two.

8. I owe the public, the shareholders, and the rest of the board the responsibility of never becoming a rubber stamp for the bank's officers.

9. The bank should expect me to have the guts to stand up against other board members should they seek to pressure management for their own benefit or that of their friends, or should they meddle in management.

No doubt you can add to this list of things which you and I owe our banks, but the above could be a starter.

On the other hand, the bank owes me a few things too.

1. I deserve to be compensated fairly for my time in board and

committee meetings, even though my acceptance of the responsibility is not for the fees I receive.

2. The bank owes me its best efforts to furnish written policy statements on all major functions of the bank, with the opportunity to review these statements periodically and to suggest changes as needed.

3. The bank owes me an opportunity to hear and see someone other than the president or chairman present reports in board meetings. At least once a year, I want to see and hear the division heads, the department heads, the principal supporting officers who are carrying out the policies of the board every day. I want to see if these men are growing, and how they perform before the board of directors. I want to question them directly, not just *in absentia* through the chairman. Besides, at least once a year, the board deserves an in-depth review of every department.

4. The bank owes me regular, meaningful reports comparing our bank with other banks in our town, in our area or state, and with banks our size in the Federal Reserve or FDIC district. These comparisons are available. I want to know whether we are as superior as the chairman and president keep telling me we are. I want to eyeball it myself.

Now, different banks make different kinds of reports to their boards. I know that some of the reports are so bulky that they are staggering and cannot possibly be reviewed and understood in the limited time boards meet each month. But in a folder before me, or else on a slide on the screen so that we can all look at the same one and talk about it at the same time, I want to review regularly or periodically all important aspects of the bank's business. This doesn't mean every month for all of them, but some monthly, some quarterly, some annually.

These are the reviews I want to see, and some I must see by law: (a) the loan account; (b) the investment account; (c) the income and expense statement, compared to budget and compared to last year's performance; (d) the major big overdrafts (if officers have violated the bank's policy on approving overdrafts, I want to find out why); (e) overdue loans; (f) officers' communications on their borrowing; and (g) I want periodically to review and appraise the more important loans in the portfolio. I prefer that such reviews come from a member of the board's loan committee. I want to know what contingent liabilities we have in the form of "courtesy" lines of credit.

These things have a habit of coming home to roost once in a while.

5. A board committee must review all types of insurance carried by the bank and present the review to me at least annually.

6. At least once a year I expect a review of operating procedures of all departments. This is best done by having one department reviewed each month; that allows plenty of months when other matters may be discussed. These reviews generally take ten or fifteen minutes, with perhaps that much discussion time; they are well worth the effort.

Now, I'm not advocating that every director spend three or four hours a day working at his job as director—it doesn't take that much time. In my bank we do it *all* with *one* regular board meeting monthly of never more than two hours, plus personal committee time of maybe four hours a month.

7. I want to see the examination reports and hear them discussed by the bank's auditor and audit committee representative. Our bank invites all interested directors to attend such a review session.

8. I want a review of the bank's liquidity position every month.

9. Once a year I want an in-depth review of the bank's growth and its projected capital needs, with recommendations for meeting those needs.

10. I want follow-up reports, on definite schedules, on any items brought to the board for decision which are special projects or new programs, such as credit cards, the opening of new areas for branching, new services, etc.

11. The bank owes the directors and our community an active program of service to the community, not only in business and industry, but also in education, cultural affairs, and political involvement of its personnel—not alone in contribution of the bank's money (although we contribute heavily), but in the taking of positions and in activity carefully calculated to be in the best interest of the bank, its customers, and the community.

12. I expect the bank to have senior officers who are willing to recognize there has to be a certain "moving over" as they grow older, to delegate responsibility to younger men, and to help them learn to make decisions; who truly allow the development of new ideas, new ways, and new people; who are willing to supervise from a little farther off as they mature and to feed in their more conservative cautions *when needed*, not just every day as a matter of course.

13. I want my bank to have executive officers who will counsel with the board of directors, but who will, on the other hand, have the stature to argue, to present facts and evidence, to maintain their position against opposition if they feel it is correct. I want an executive officer who will insist on managing and who will insist on the board's staying in its policy-making role, but who will, likewise, gracefully reassess his position when shown that he, too, is only one board member where bank policy is concerned.

14. The bank owes me the courtesy of giving me time enough in board meetings to review, to question, to understand. That is not to say that I should be allowed to require a board committee to go all over again through all matters it has considered in arriving at its recommendation to the board; but I should be allowed to satisfy myself that the committee has had the facts, has considered them carefully, and has made a policy recommendation that is reasonable, even though I might not have done it exactly the same way.

15. The bank owes me protection, either by bank indemnification in the by-laws or by insurance, from malicious or nuisance or unjustified shareholders' suits so common today.

16. The bank owes me periodic discussions of national trends in bank organization, bank corporate structure, and directions, and should keep me generally informed of major legislative proposals which may if enacted into law substantially affect my bank and my investment in it.

My purpose here has been to deal with common sense and reasonable care. The language of the courts on these matters is easily understood, and I believe the concepts contained in their decisions underlie all our responsibilities as directors. Such are the things which go along with the honor of serving as a bank director. That is why, as a bank director, I expect from the executives of my bank enough information, reports, and opportunity for *involvement* to insure that I can reasonably carry out these responsibilities.

I like very much what a former deputy comptroller of the currency —and a state superintendent of banks—once said:

> The welfare of an entire community may well depend on the quality and responsibility of bank directors. . . . I strongly believe that the best way we have of lifting our banking system to new heights of soundness and service to our people is by drawing directors more closely and thoroughly into the responsibilities of policy formation. . . . The surface of their ability and willingness to help banking

has hardly been scratched. Directors are the great reserve of strength in the banking business. We must try harder than we have to extract from directors the unlimited measure of wisdom and guidance that they may give.

Certainly the Assemblies for Bank Directors offer us that opportunity.

EUGENE L. SWEARINGEN

Evaluating the Quality of Bank Management

A VERY WISE BANK PRESIDENT once said that the first item on the agenda of every board of directors is the question, Shall we retain the chief executive officer? "Whether we put it on the agenda or not," he said, "this is the first thing that should be thought about each time we have a board of directors meeting." He said that if the answer is "No," then the next question is "What procedure shall we use to select the new chief executive officer, and who will be on the committee to do it?" And if the answer is "Yes, we shall retain the chief executive officer," the next question is, "OK, how can we help him do his job?"

We are talking about every board of directors' number one job. If you have the wrong president, it is your responsibility to correct that. If you have the right man, then many of your other problems will not be as difficult to solve, because you have faith in the quality of that person. There are some twenty questions which I think you can use either to evaluate your chief executive officer or, if you are the chief executive officer, to evaluate your own performance. If you have to go out and find a chief executive, then these are the kinds of questions you should be asking yourself about this person:

1. What qualities do you want in your chief executive officer? This depends upon the area of the country you come from, upon the size of your bank, and upon an analysis of the job that you expect of that man. Do you want a person who is to be primarily a manager, or a person who is to be a chief loan officer? I have found that the primary mistake made in banking is taking a person who is competent in one job and promoting him to his level of incompetence as president (the best example I have ever seen of the "Peter Principle"). You tend to do this because you evaluate a man on his performance as a loan officer, or on the fact that he has more seniority in the bank than anyone

else, or on the fact that he has been an excellent person to head your trust department, and therefore conclude that he can be the manager of your bank. Well, I would rather have as my president a person who is a great leader than a person who has proven that he is a great follower of someone else.

Sometimes a person gets into the position of leadership simply because he has been an excellent Man Friday for the man who preceded him as president. I suggest that you as a director read both *The Peter Principle* and the second book which Dr. Peter wrote, *The Peter Prescription.* Dr. Peter developed the principle that a man tends to be promoted until he reaches his level of incompetence, and then he spends the rest of his life in that position. This led a lot of people to write in and ask Dr. Peter, "Well, how in the world do we keep from promoting a man to his level of incompetence?" or "How do I keep from getting promoted to my level of incompetence?" *The Peter Prescription* contains about sixty-four suggestions as to how to keep from being promoted into a job where you will be incompetent.

2. How well does this man who is to be president understand himself? Many years ago Socrates said, "Know thyself." I have heard many people say, "You make me sick." What we really should say is, "I make me sick." Now you may have behavior which I don't like, but I should be in control of my own behavior. I should control my own adrenal glands. If your behavior causes me to become sick, it is because of me—not because of you. And so if you are going to put a certain man in charge of your bank, one of the first questions I would ask is, "Is he in control of himself?" I would not want to put a person in charge of a bank who had a reputation for losing control of himself through drinking, or loss of temper, or anything else. If he isn't in control of himself, I don't think he is going to be a very good president of your bank.

3. How cooperative is this man? He is going to have to work with a board. He is going to have to work with other community leaders. He is going to have to attempt to build a team, and for the first time in his life it may be that he is going to have to get the job done through other people. Now this is what separates a manager from a man who is just a top loan officer or a top man in his particular niche. The loan officer, in many cases, has never supervised anybody but a secretary. In many cases he sat across the desk from somebody who had to attempt to sell him on a loan. One of his primary abilities was

to analyze situations and thus to make good loans. Now he is going to have to turn a lot of this work over to someone else and get the job done through teamwork. And so the problem is, Is he going to be cooperative?

4. What viewpoint is he going to take in making decisions? I know of a man who was an excellent dean of a School of Engineering. This man never became president of a university because he saw the university's problems only from the point of view of the School of Engineering. Now, one of the difficulties with banks, as I have seen it, is that we tend to teach a man more and more about less and less, and the bigger we get as a bank, the more we specialize this individual. He starts out as a loan officer, and then he becomes a commercial loan officer, and then after deciding what industry he is going to specialize in he begins to think that there is nothing more important than, say, making a petroleum loan in his bank. If he begins to believe that his corner of the office represents the entire corporation, then he is not going to make a good president. You should look for that man who understands that his point of view has to be broad enough so that he can see the problem from other people's points of view. If a particular man has not demonstrated the fact that he can look beyond his own point of view and realize that he is causing trouble for someone else, then he is not going to make a good president.

5. Does he really like people as individuals? I want to suggest to you that banking is a people business. I believe this. Of course, we are dealing with money; but our money is just like the money of the bank down the street. The difference between one bank and another is primarily in the quality of the people. Ours is a service industry, and we must provide this service in a way that pleases the customer. Ultimately, if we fail to please the customer we are going to go out of business.

Profits are the by-products of the efficient rendering of a service which the customer needs; if you can render this service, then you are going to make profits. Now I have heard bankers say, "I am in business to make a profit." I don't think that is what you are in business for. I don't think that justifies your existence as a corporation, or even your existence as an individual. Profits are absolutely necessary; if you don't make them, you can't stay in business. But the thing that justifies your stay in business is the fact that you realize you have to render a service to people; therefore, I would want a person as president who is sensitive to the feelings of other people, a person who likes to deal with other people and to be of service to them.

6. What is his philosophy about the nature of man? Many of you have seen the little glass that has a cartoon of a man with the corners of his mouth turned down; the man is saying, "People are no damn good!" Now if you believe that people are no damn good, you are not going to make a good bank president. I want my bank president to believe that people are some damn good, that people do amount to something, that they are worth something. If you believe that most people are basically honest, that they want to be good, that they want to be productive, that they want to meet their obligations, then I think you are going to have a philosophy about the nature of man which will enable you to work well with your employees. I don't think you are going to be a good supervisor unless you have a great deal of faith in human nature. If you believe basically that your employees are out to steal from you, that they don't want to render any service, that they don't like being productive, that they will cheat on the time they give you every chance they get, then you are not going to inspire these people to produce the best for your organization.

7. Will he give credit to other people? I think that one of the things I would want to know is whether or not a person tries to get the glory for everything that is accomplished and places the blame upon everyone else when something goes wrong. A good president has to be a person who will assume the responsibility for something that goes wrong in his organization, but who has enough courage to turn over to other people the jobs that must be done, recognizing that they may make mistakes. If you are the kind of person who will not allow your employees to make mistakes, then you can't run a big organization.

8. What about the integrity of this individual? Recently the newspapers carried a story of a bank president who had stolen money down through the years. Not once did this person ever indicate that this was against any of his principles. Stealing had seemed like a game to him. Somebody once said, "He who stands for nothing will fall for anything." I would like to ask about any prospective president's character. What kind of person is he? Will he steal from your organization? Not only that, but what kind of person is he in many other ways? A banker has to stand for integrity and character in his bank. When a bank loses its reputation for integrity it is in real trouble, and

therefore the quality of the integrity and leadership of the top man is going to be important to your bank.

9. Will he keep on learning? To ask a man who is forty-five years old and being considered for the presidency of your bank where he graduated, what he took in college, etc., is about as ridiculous as to ask a high-school graduate whether he majored in sandbox one or sandbox two.

The thing that is important about a man is whether or not he keeps on learning, not what he did in a college program. In fact, if his college didn't teach him that he will have to keep on learning all his life, then he didn't get a very good education. In a very basic sense, we are learning something every day we are in a banking organization, or in any other progressive organization, and if you don't keep on learning you are going to be behind the times pretty soon. And so I would want to ask the question, "How sincere is this person about studying?" It is amazing to me that I spend more hours reading now as a bank president than I did when I was a university president. A university president is an ex-scholar; but in a bank there is an amazing amount of material coming across your desk every day, and you are going to have to try to keep up with your profession.

10. Will this man listen effectively? It is interesting to me that the farther up you go in an organization, the less you get to talk and the more you have to listen. Now this is contrary to the nature of man. I just love to talk, and therefore one of the greatest problems I have is recognizing the fact that much of the information I must get has to come from other people. I no longer have first-line contact with all of the problems. I have to listen to an analysis of a loan. I have to listen to a story about a human relations problem. I have to spend a great deal of time listening. Listening is not just a function of the ear. Listening is a function of the eyes, of the mind, of the heart, if you like. You have to have empathy for people. You have to be willing to sit back and listen to this person and ask not only what he is saying, but what he means. The ability to listen, I think, is extremely important. Can he get information accurately by listening?

11. Is he effective in planning? One of the most important responsibilities of the chief executive officer is to assist in settting the goals and objectives of his organization. He cannot delegate this job to someone else. If you are the chief executive officer, the direction of movement of your bank, the basic philosophy of your bank, is your

responsibility (with the board of directors), and there is no way you can get out of that job. Determine whether this man has proven himself to be a good planner. Has he set goals for himself and for the organization, and has he measured his performance against these goals? If he has done this sort of thing, then he would probably carry over the practice in his job as president.

You should get people to set goals and objectives and to recognize that these must be continually updated. We need short-range goals and we need goals of intermediate range—that is, a range of three to five years. When we decided to build a new building we had to ask ourselves, "Are we going to own it, or are we going to lease space in it?" We decided we didn't want to tie up that amount of capital in a building, so we decided to lease space in our new building. We had to look fifteen, twenty, or twenty-five years down the road in order to answer this kind of question. Then you must recognize that planning is a process that goes on all the time and is constantly changing. Plans are always subject to review. You have to compare your performance with the plans and ask yourself whether your assumptions are still valid.

Let me suggest to you that planning is a very rigorous discipline imposed upon an organization. For example, in our bank we have about $295 million in loans. If we reach the goals of our five-year plan, we know we are going to have over $500 million in loans. Now this tells us something about the number of loan officers we are going to need. It tells us something about the training of these people that has to be done. It tells us not only about the people we have to replace, but about the new ones we have to bring in and train in order to accomplish this job. Finally, if conditions change, if money becomes tight when we thought it was not going to be so tight, then obviously these changes must be taken into consideration.

12. Does he get facts before reaching a conclusion? I would hope that this person would have a reputation for waiting until he had all of the information that he could assemble. Now, you never have all you *want*. In every loan we make we wish we knew more about certain things. But in most cases, you think, "I have gotten all of the information that is readily available; this man has to have an answer." (I think banks make a terrible mistake in postponing an answer, particularly one that is going to be unfavorable. This just makes a man madder than ever when he gets an answer.) I think many times we

don't make the decision at the right time, but there are some people who make the decision without getting the facts they need to make it properly.

13. What kind of an image will this man project for your bank? There is no escaping the fact that the bank's chief executive officer does project an image: an image of enthusiasm, or an image of lethargy. I know a bank president who projects the image of a man who plays gin almost all day in his bank. If a correspondent banker wants to call upon him, he drops in and they play gin for a while. That bank is not going any place at this time and hasn't for several years. The image that is being projected there is not an image of a dynamic, moving bank.

You can have other kinds of images. I am not telling you what kind you should have. I think that is up to the board of directors. You may want to project an image of a very conservative bank. You may want to be very dynamic. You may want to be a bank that is interested in growth. You may want to be one that is more interested in shareholders' profits. That is for you to decide. But I will tell you this: the man you select to be the chief executive officer will have a great influence on the kind of image that your bank projects.

14. Is this man effective in delegation? There is no way to run a big organization except by delegation, and some people will not delegate because they fear losing authority. Or they think, "If I delegate, somebody is going to make a mistake, and then I will be blamed for it." *An insecure man cannot delegate.* Show me a good delegator, and I will show you a man who has faith in himself and faith in his people. If he doesn't have that, he can't turn the job over to someone else. Not only do you have to turn the job over to someone else, but you have to follow through to see if it is being done. Now, one of the main responsibilities of a bank president is to see to it that there is a control and information system in his organization that enables him to know whether or not the job is being done. Your president may fear losing job satisfaction. I have seen people who will not turn over the job of making loans, primarily because they like making loans. They would rather do that than anything else. They are secure in that, and so they don't quite understand the job of managing the whole thing. They keep on doing what they understand well, and that may not be the job that they ought to be doing.

And so I would ask the question about your chief executive officer,

Is he doing things right, or is he doing the right things? I think we make more mistakes sometimes by doing the wrong things right than we do by simply fouling up on what we are doing. Let me make one other point about competency. You are never going to have an organization fouled up by a total incompetent. The people who will foul up an organization are the people who are competent in something and get promoted into a position where they are incompetent. The thing that fouls up an organization is a nice guy who is incompetent at what he is doing, and a manager who doesn't have the guts to remove him from that position.

15. Is this man effective in communication? Can he get up in front of your Rotary Club and make a talk about your bank? Can he talk about what's going on in the economy? Can he use words effectively? He doesn't have to have the world's greatest vocabulary. I have seen people in the Southwest who could really communicate in a few words, and that is what is important. Dan Devine tells a story of a coach grabbing a great big tackle off the bench one day and saying, "Get in there and get rambunctious." Well, he starts onto the field, hesitates, and then comes back and says, "What's his number, coach?"

16. What about his brain power and his judgment? Now I don't care what his education is, but I want a smart person leading my bank. I want a man who can understand and analyze an issue and who has sound judgment in arriving at a decision, a man who will work smarter, not harder. There is a little poem that goes like this:

> We have two ends with a common link.
> On one we sit; with one we think.
> Success depends on which we use;
> It's a case of heads we win and tails we lose.

17. Does he know how to organize a team? And does he know how to organize himself? I think it is very important that this person be able to use his time effectively. There are going to be a lot of people wanting his time, and he has to decide where he is going to spend this very limited resource, the time that is available to him.

18. Can he select the right people and correct the mistakes that he makes? Now I do not expect a chief executive officer always to select the right person, but if he makes a mistake and the man doesn't work out, then I expect him to have enough guts to correct the mistake he

made. This is terribly important. He does have the responsibility for judging the performance of other people. Now, notice I said judging the *performance* of other people, not judging *people*. I will leave that to the Lord. But judging the performance of people is our job.

19. How do people work with and for him? How effective is he in motivating the work of other people? I used to tell students about the track coach that had a lousy pole vaulter. He was so bad that the track coach thought he was going to lose the track meet because of him. But the pole vaulter backed into the javelin thrower and won the broad jump. I don't know what it takes to motivate people. I think more and more it is what I would call, or what psychologists are calling, self-actualization or self-fulfillment. I know this: you can't depend now just upon the threat of firing somebody. You will never get the best response out of people unless somehow or other you can analyze what makes this individual tick. What does he want out of life? What is it that will cause him to turn on for an organization?

20. Is he flexible? Can he adjust to change? There is a story of a ninety-year-old man who was asked at his birthday party if he had seen a lot of changes in his life. He said, "Yes, and I have been against every damn one of them." Now, there are people like this who don't want to adjust to change. But flexibility and the capacity to adjust to change are essential qualities for good leadership.

CHARLES M. VAN HORN

The Bank Management Gap

THE RECORD OF ACHIEVEMENT of the commercial banking industry, especially since 1960, is truly notable. A never-ending stream of innovations has provided a vast and growing market with a striking variety of high-quality financial facilities and services. Despite extensive mechanization and computerization, the number of employees in the industry doubled between 1955 and 1971. This period of unparalleled banking expansion has created a management gap not only at the chief executive officer level but in middle management as well. The problem is not a new one, but as bank functions become more complex and expansion accelerates, there are indications that the shortage of management talent is becoming more acute.

During the last decade, while the application of computers and related technology was the central concern, the development of our human resources was somewhat neglected. Talented executives, not complex computer hardware or eye-catching branch offices, are at the heart of the service industry you represent. Despite all the recent advances in techniques and technology, banking effectiveness depends primarily on well-qualified bankers.

A review of the latest reports of examination reveals that about one-half of New York State's national banks lack competent successor management to take the place of the incumbents. In calling your attention to this fact, I am not suggesting that the problem is limited to the Empire State. It is not confined to any one geographical area of the United States. For example, a 1969 survey by the Federal Reserve Bank of Philadelphia found that one out of five Third District reporting bankers either had a management succession problem at the time or anticipated one within the next five years.

The lack of a capable successor would not be of serious consequence if the bank could easily attract a replacement when the need arises. However, the pool of available management talent is shallow and banks are experiencing increasing difficulty in attracting personnel from that source.

To trace the evolution of the bank management gap, we must go back a generation. No significant new blood entered banking from the beginning of the Great Depression until after the end of World War II. This was a period of retrenchment and "holding the fort." In the 1940s many competent and promising bankers left for improved salaries and job opportunities outside the industry. There was an influx of "capable young management people" in the 1950s, but timid men, scarred by the trauma of the 1930s, suppressed many of these recruits or drove them out.

Since 1960 there has been a vast upsurge in banking activities. Just to mention one indicator, the total number of banking offices in New York increased more than 53 percent in the last decade. The "soaring '60s" saw banks move into new fields and introduce new services on a scale and with a speed not previously witnessed. These efforts to meet the needs of an increasingly sophisticated public dramatically intensified the need for bank management personnel.

Despite the progress of the more recent past, the banking industry has had to live down its earlier reputation for stodginess and lack of opportunity. Although the period when these forces prevailed is well behind us, it takes time to establish a new image.

The quality of bank management today is higher than it has ever been. In general, managers are better educated and better trained than their predecessors. The problem is one of quantity; there are too few capable individuals to fill positions of responsibility in banks today and in the foreseeable future. The ranks of middle management, a logical source of top management candidates, are extremely thin.

Many of the larger banks and holding companies, as well as the smaller banks, are in quest of management talent. As the need becomes more acute, competitors in the immediate service area are likely to offer ever higher salaries and incentives for the management skills which are in short supply.

Both before and since the passage of the Bank Merger Act of 1960, the problem of management succession has been cited as a major factor in merger efforts. Perhaps half of the bank mergers in recent years have involved management deficiencies.

The formation and expansion of holding companies has been suggested as one way of dealing with the gap; however, this is not always the solution, as the larger lead bank may not have the right person for the job when the vacancy occurs. Furthermore, in their training programs the lead banks in the multibank holding companies tend to develop specialists in various areas rather than the well-rounded generalists which smaller banks require.

Personnel released when some of the major banks reduced their staffs have found opportunities in other banks; however, as cost-cutting reaches its limits, with improvement in the national economy, fewer replacements can be counted on from this source.

Any consideration of the factors which have contributed to the continuing management shortage must include a reference to bankers who were on their way to the top when they took a detour to John Barleycorn's office. Alcoholism is one of the country's most serious medical and social problems. It is reported that 80 percent of the nation's alcoholics are between 30 and 50 years of age; therefore, it is a potential problem at all levels of management.

If the job performance of a federal civilian employee is impaired by misuse of alcohol, the law now requires that treatment and rehabilitation programs and services be provided for him. Now here is something for all of us to keep in mind: according to Dr. Ralph Fingar—Chief, Psychology Service, Veterans Administration Hospital, Boston—any amount in excess of four ounces of alcohol a day, on average, is beyond what is considered intelligent drinking. Managers, supervisors, and employees alike need further education in recognizing alcoholism as an illness.

Each bank has a part to play in filling the management gap. Management development is not a luxury which only big banks can afford. For banks of all sizes, management development represents both a necessity and an opportunity. Banks need not fear that they may develop an excessive number of bank officers.

The search for qualified leadership should begin in your own bank. I suggest that you take a comprehensive inventory of the human resources of the bank. Evaluate the performance of each employee and estimate his or her potential. Afford promising employees the opportunity for self-development. Involve them in the process of management; merely rotating them among departments is not enough. Beyond formal education in the tools of management, leaders are developed by practice. Ask subordinates what *they* think before you tell them what *you* think. Good questioning can lead them to understand your position and to speak honestly on theirs. Responsibilities need to be delegated and rewarded accordingly. The management development program in banking requires that all be challenged to growth and self-development.

One of the deficiencies we have observed in bank training programs is the tendency to place too much emphasis on the development of specialists at the expense of the development of generalists. This could and should be alleviated by rotation of duties of management-caliber personnel, supplemented by formal training programs involving the duties of the chief executive officer. This is indeed an age of specialization in banking, but in the larger banks this does not have to mean "once a mortgage officer, always a mortgage officer." While not all employees might be qualified for such broad-based training, certainly those with ambition, drive, and ability should be given the opportunity.

Recruitment efforts must cast a much wider net today than in an earlier era. The Civil Rights Act of 1964 prohibits job discrimination because of "race, color, religion, sex or national origin." Even if there were no such law, the facts of the current labor force situation would call for the scrapping of some old-fashioned banking traditions.

Women comprise over three-fifths of all bank employees—compared with only one-fifth as recently as the eve of World War II. Yet in 1969 only 10 percent of bank officers were women, while in other business fields the ratio was approximately 15 percent. The situation appears to be improving, but womanpower represents a virtually untapped pool of potential management talent from which banks may draw in the years ahead.

To this day, the ranks of senior management in many banks are filled only by senior citizens. Among the three hundred largest banks, however, the median age of the bank president in 1969 was forty-nine, two years younger than the median age in 1963. The trend is likely to continue. Not long ago a thirty-four year-old was made president of a major Atlanta bank.

One holding company organization recently appointed eight new presidents and six executive vice-presidents, all in their thirties or early forties. The policy is to give promising young persons important jobs to "let them develop fast—or go somewhere else." The arbitrary setting of a lower limit of forty-five to fifty on the age of a chief executive officer of a bank cannot be justified. After all, the American Constitution entrusts the presidency of the United States to a thirty-five year-old. With more and more executives taking early retirement, more young persons will be taking over the reins in banking.

The banking industry is to be commended for developing formal training programs on a scale which few industries can match. The Executive Management School sponsored by the New York State Bankers Association, the Arden House Program in Bank Management, the various graduate schools of banking, the American Institute of Banking, and the wide variety of educational programs under the sponsorship of the American Bankers Association are all meritorious educational enterprises. For the most part, however, these programs are specialized and too brief.

The need for a "Bank Presidential Preparation Program" is more urgent today than it was seven years ago. Such a program would be designed to turn out large numbers of well-trained individuals to replenish the management pool. It would call for the close cooperation of bankers and educational leaders. This might be accomplished by altering existing M.B.A. programs to include more of the practical side of banking. As it is, there are only a handful of universities which offer an M.B.A. program in banking. Intelligent young men and women with drive and initiative might be selected for the program regardless of prior educational attainments. The benefits to be derived from such a program would far outweigh the costs, direct and indirect, of the employees' participation in the program for a year or so.

Too often bankers are complacent about the management succession problem, continuing to believe that they can go out and buy whatever executives they need. This traditional approach is not realistic today for two reasons. First, successors are not as readily available as heretofore. Second, even if top management could be located, the earnings of many banks might not support current and prospective salary levels. During the past two years we have noted a sharp increase in salaries offered to candidates for the chief executive officer position in newly-chartered national banks not affiliated with another bank or holding company. The typical starting salary is $35,000 per annum, up from $25,000 two years ago. Within the past year, two relatively new national banks have been actively recruiting to fill the chief executive officer position at a salary of $35,000 per annum or more. In one of those instances the position was filled after an eight-month search. In the other, after the board of directors interviewed many candidates over a period of eighteen months without success, they decided to merge into another institution.

A 1969 study completed for the Association of Reserve City Bankers showed that even in larger banks, salaries, including incentive payments, were behind those of industrial firms. Needless to say, effective competition for qualified manpower requires a further narrowing in the total compensation pattern.

Moreover, median compensation of the second highest paid bank officer was 71 percent of the compensation of the top banker in larger institutions last year, whereas in manufacturing the ratio was 74 percent. In the mid '60s the ratio in banking was under 50 percent. Here, too, banks have come a long way, but there is room for further improvement.

Our office conducted a survey of all national banks in the Second Region as of August 31, 1972. It revealed that among the forty-three national banks in New York State with assets from $10 to $25 million, median top pay was $25,400, while the second highest officer received $18,000. The twenty-one banks with assets from $25 to $50 million averaged $29,300 for the top executive, and $23,200 for the number two officer. Among the twenty-three national banks in the $50 to $100 million asset class, the top officer's median salary was $37,000, while the number two officer's salary was $26,000. These figures are significantly higher than they were a few years ago.

Some of the regulatory agencies have experienced the same personnel problems with which the banks are confronted. The Officer of the Comptroller of the Currency has actively sought to attract and retain capable personnel. Efforts include on-campus recruiting, on-the-job training supplemented by formal schooling, rapid promotion to positions of responsibility, and a compensation schedule competitive with other sectors of the economy. The 1973 starting salary for assistant national bank examiners is $9,500. Commissioned national bank examiners earn as much as $35,000.

In a rapidly moving economy, the banking industry must regularly revise the compensation package to attract and retain high-quality personnel. Some of you may be thinking at this point, "But we can't afford to pay higher management salaries." My only reply is that you can't afford not to offer executive compensation which is competitive within banking, as well as with other industries.

Banking in the '70s faces continuing change and repeated challenges. Fresh ideas and concepts will be needed. Young people drawn from all groups in our society should find it attractive to meet the challenge of growing with an industry which continues to renew, revitalize, and expand itself. By recruiting vigorously, compensating adequately, training thoroughly, and giving youth a chance to assume responsibilities as rapidly as their abilities warrant, bankers can fill the management gap and realize the promising potential of banking.

PHILIP E. COLDWELL

Appraisal and Planning

THE DIRECTORS of any organization—whether a commercial bank, a nonbank financial institution, or a nonfinancial institution—have a responsibility to their organization to insure that the management is doing a proper job of planning ahead and appraising all the relevant factors which impinge upon each of the planning problems. This is not to say that the directors should be involved at a level which infringes upon management's prerogatives. But, as with many other facets of directors' work, they should keep themselves well informed of the progress of management and insure that management is, in fact, doing the job of planning, not only for short- and intermediate-term projects, but also for long-range situations. More specifically, a director's responsibility includes seeing that management is taking appropriate steps in the direction of time and personnel toward long-range planning, and is keeping the directors adequately informed as well as availing itself of the expertise of men on the board of directors in seeking the solution of long-range problems.

Perhaps we can place this discussion in the context of some of the problems which your banks should be considering. For example, is your bank management planning and considering the future for changes in the structure of banking in your state? Structural changes include the new holding company law and its impact, potential changes in branch regulations, effects of the holding company structure upon branching and unit bank operations, and the potentials (both favorable and unfavorable) of organizing a bank holding company.

Since it is apparent that in a longer-range context some of the present nonbank financial institutions may obtain banking authority and could become strong and vital competitors on the local banking scene, is your bank management planning ahead to consider new competition?

Of course, there is a wide range of forward planning necessary in management succession, personnel assignments, potential unionization and personnel responses to such unionization, and the continuing job of keeping the salary and fringe-benefits of the bank's employees abreast of those in the community as a whole.

I plan to focus my attention, however, upon what the directors should be considering in the field of economic and financial planning. I hope to point out to you some of the things which directors can do to assist their managements in better forward planning of loan commitments, revenue and deposit sources, shifting economic bases of your community and banking responses thereto, and, in a much broader sense, economic planning in adjusting to the changing circumstances and conditions reflected in the national markets and the effects these have upon bank profitability.

As directors, you have outside contacts in your own business and through your own associations providing information and attitudes which should be of immense help to the officers of your banks in developing their own ideas about the changing environment of the nation and the shifting markets for financial instruments. Perhaps more important, you as directors should be having monthly discussions with your managements on the way in which the financial environment is developing, on any new trends which seem to be on the horizon, and on how your own personal appraisal of these trends might influence your banks' operations. You should be counseling with the managements of your banks on all aspects of future economic planning, making sure that your banks' officers have the data which are regularly published and available in the public arena. You should be encouraging them to maintain a continuing awareness and interest in the status of the financial markets and the economic markets of their primary customers, reaching toward consultant help through your correspondents, through the services of the Federal Reserve and other regulatory agencies, and, of course, through regular news letters of financial consultants.

Probably of equal importance is the application of common sense. Despite the broad changes in banking and financial affairs of the nation, there are certain repetitive patterns which develop over the business cycle and over the financial cycle response to changes in the growth rate of the nation. It is important that your managements recognize these repetitive patterns, learning that a change in the objective targets of monetary policy toward a restraining policy can forecast a reduced availability of credit, a slower rate of deposit growth, an eventual problem of liquidity, and certainly a rising pattern of interest rates. I would caution you, though, to modify your judgments to take into account some of the new elements in the situation, particularly the availability of nondeposit sources of funds, but to base your modifications on your own banks' situation. Do not merely follow the leaders, i.e., your correspondents or the national money market banks. What may be appropriate for a large city bank participating in some of these nondeposit sources could be wholly inappropriate for a bank in a different situation. As I review the developments over the past three years and my contacts with boards of directors, I find that too few have spent time with the managements of their banks in trying to forecast the coming changes in financial markets, even though some changes were clearly predicted in the trends of Federal Reserve monetary policies, the nation's fiscal policies, and the published economic and financial data.

It is, of course, not only desirable from a citizenship standpoint, but also a requirement for a bank director to know something of the workings of the nation's central bank. The Federal Reserve System is charged with responsibility for developing monetary policy. Its objective is to provide a supply of credit compatible with the demand which will support a high-level utilization of resources at reasonable price stability. The Federal Reserve is also involved in a number of other matters, but its monetary policy work is the prime mission of the System. The Reserve Board and the banks have discount rates, reserve requirements, and open market operations to accomplish their policy rquirements, with the latter one being most heavily used in both a day-to-day and an overall implementation basis.

The central feature of the System's responsibility for monetary policy is the power to create and extinguish bank reserves. It is this power which makes any central bank of prime importance in the economic stabilization of the nation. Perhaps one small example will help explain my point:

If the Open Market Committee decides that additional reserves must be created to improve the supply of credit in the nation, it instructs the manager of the open market account in New York to purchase government securities. After a brief go-round with the dealers in government securities, the open market desk decides upon the best price available and purchases, say, $100 million worth of such securities. It places the order with a dealer and, assuming regular delivery, receives those securities the next day and pays for them by check. The dealer, of course, is not interested in holding the check, so he quickly deposits it with his commercial bank. That bank, in turn, wanting to obtain the funds represented by the check, takes it back to the Federal Reserve Bank of New York, which then credits the reserve account of the commercial bank. At this point in the procedure, the Federal Reserve has purchased $100 million worth of government securities and has paid for them by check. Now, where did the money come from? Well, obviously, it came by creation of credit by the Federal Reserve. Its final step was to credit the reserve account of the commercial bank.

But suppose that commercial bank wanted cash or currency instead. This would present no problem, because the Federal Reserve issues and distributes the currency of the nation, and it could pay the commercial bank $100 million in currency. If the New York Federal Reserve's stock should run low, it could merely ask the Bureau of Engraving and Printing to print up a new batch. It is this central authority to create credit, backed by the authority to distribute currency, that makes the central bank such a powerful instrument.

For those of you who wish to keep track of Federal Reserve changes in policy, there are published every week data indicating the level of reserves, the changes in those reserves, and the open market operations as reflected in the books of the Federal Reserve banks. You should, of course, be extremely careful in making judgments from short-run data. Take a longer look over a quarter or several months, and I believe you can discern the trend of Federal Reserve policy. The policy, of course, is not as precise as the data, but for your purposes in guiding and directing a commercial bank, the trend of policy is the important factor.

Perhaps some of this has been evident to me because of the rather routine method some banks have of holding one-hour directors' meetings once a month in which management reviews the conditions of the bank and some of its important credit lines, but seldom gets into a thorough discussion of the planning and forward thinking management should be doing in preparation for the changes which are just over the horizon. While we can blame management for not doing its job,

I submit that it is also, at least partly, the fault of the directors of the bank in failing to encourage management to take a longer view, and failing to participate in committee work or board action to insure the careful appraisal of longer-term and even short-run economic financial trends.

Even in states such as Texas where the banking structure is oriented toward a unit-banking law, the growth of chain and holding company banking is such that virtually every bank in the state should be carefully appraising the impact of the developing structural shifts, studying the value of group versus chain or unit banking, and observing the impact of these two upon the viability of a unit-banking law. Thus, you as directors and owners of the banks should be appraising your position, both as to whether it is desirable to join in such a group and as to what your competitive reaction would be if your competitor down the street should make such a move.

Another intermediate- to long-range problem is related to the pattern of community or national economic and business development. It is seldom that the basic sources of economic growth shift rapidly in a single community. The more usual pattern is a one-to-five-year cycle of the development of a new industry, and the growth of that industry's credit needs which will have to be accommodated by a financial institution. It took a number of years for the cattle feedlot industry in West Texas to develop, but the financial institutions of that area needed to look carefully at both the capital and the operating requirements of that industry to appraise the part their banks could play in supplying this credit and the part others in the financial arena might absorb.

To maintain the competitive position of banks among all financial institutions, it is highly desirable and almost imperative that the banks maintain a forward look toward the development of new economic growth patterns, and appraise the banks' responsibility and response to new business development. Perhaps one example will suffice. Many banks are presently involved in credit card operations, but those which are not so involved need to appraise carefully the operational, credit, and lendable fund impact of this new credit device. To the somewhat larger banks, their planning horizons should now include preauthorized payment plans, for it seems certain that over the next ten years there will be a major movement toward reducing the number of checks being passed through the financial community, and it appears that preauthorized payment plans offer one viable means of at least partially accomplishing this end. Among the variety of things a bank must consider are costs, returns, volatility of deposits generated, if any, the volatility and lack of control over loan demand in the credit card area, the operational needs in a computer and personnel sense, and the legal and corporate requirements which may be necessary in the establishment of preauthorized payment plans.

In looking at your bank management and at your bank in the overall financial community, you as directors should be using the following checklist:

1. Is your bank planning ahead, and do you have a directors' committee or a board of directors' mandate both to contribute to and to appraise the results of your management's planning efforts?

2. Are you participating in the future planning of your bank, contributing your knowledge of the developing trends in local industry (both present and potential), and contributing your personal appraisal of the longer-range economic and financial developments?

3. Do you personally try to stay abreast of the published data to judge the next turn in financial affairs?

4. Do you have a regular discussion with your bank management on the forward trends of the economy and the management's response to these trends?

5. Is there a time in your board meetings when bank management will report the results of its forward planning and lay out its policy moves to adjust your bank's operations to the anticipated conditions?

6. Do you encourage your management to participate in analysis of costs, such as the Federal Reserve Functional Cost Program?

7. Do you as directors participate in the planning of the bank for financial structure changes and for major changes in service to customers?

If your answers to these questions are in the affirmative, and if you aid your bank management in solving its forward-planning programs, I think you will find that your bank is moving ahead of your competitor, because too few banks in the nation are doing enough long-range planning.

RONALD A. TERRY

Managing Resources

WE HAVE TWO BASIC RESOURCES available to us in the banking industry —money and people. A discussion of the management of either financial or human resources is far too broad a subject to cover in depth in so brief an essay, so only an outline of some basic considerations will be attempted.

The management of financial resources concerns itself with the rate differential on flows of funds through our banks—with the name of the game being to maintain an adequate spread between the rates paid for the items on the liability side of the balance sheet and the return on the assets.

Of course, we are learning to generate income from sources other than the spread of our funds flows, but this rate differentiation will remain the backbone of banking income and deserves our prime consideration.

The basic problem of our industry is that the spreads we maintain are difficult to increase and probably will decrease in our controlled environment. Therefore, with expenses growing rapidly in our people-intensive business, we have had to turn to the generation of increased volume to maintain profit margins. Increases in volume have made our earnings very susceptible to changes in money rates, and the last five years have proved to be difficult times for asset and liability managers to maintain a balanced balance sheet, proper liquidity, and satisfactory earnings.

What we need is more stability in the activities where our funds are used, and also more types of acceptable risks in the financial areas and hence more return on our shareholders' investments. Your managers are controlling flows of dollars through your bank. They can pretty well control the number of dollars to handle, and I think there are about five basic rules that haven't changed concerning the management of these dollars:

1. Think long term.
2. Preserve your liquidity.
3. Be prepared for the unexpected—since you are used as the basic tool of monetary policy.
4. Don't be myopic about your accounting periods and make bad investment decisions for the sole purpose of making a year or a quarter look good.
5. Plow enough back into your community to maintain the foundation for your growth.

Consumers and the public are demanding these days that corporations act like good citizens, and any bank with a resource management program that results in a fat profit today and a lousy town tomorrow is destroying the hand that feeds it.

I am not suggesting we pour some of the stockholders' money down the drain. No one is more sensitive to the earnings on each of his stockholders' shares than I am. This is the very essence of management responsibility. However, my keen awareness that there is no other place for any of our banks to do business except in their own town leads me to the inevitable conclusion that unless we can reconcile the profit responsibility and social responsibility, we may sacrifice our franchises to someone in the financial sector who can.

If directors are going to perpetuate the growth of their banks, they will do so by insisting on a positive program of human resource management.

There are a lot of revolutions occurring now—technology, knowledge, population, education—which are forcing a reassessment of management styles. We are caught up in the technological progress of computers and information handling. We are faced with potential obsolescence everywhere.

The growth of knowledge is thrusting so much reading material on our desks every day that it is impossible to absorb. We all share the frustration of trying to decide what to read and never feeling that we've done enough.

The population explosion has resulted in half the people in the country being under twenty-seven, and many of them think they can't "trust anybody over thirty."

Some of the best-educated people in history are working today, and their expectations are on the rise, for they know there is a good life available.

History has taught us a lot about management. Man's first management style was one of coercion and fear, in which a subordinate, like a galley slave, faced punishment for not getting the job done. Things got done, but not very efficiently. Then came the style of authority and obedience, prevalent in armed services today, where orders were issued to be carried out. Built on authority and power, it proved a little more efficient than merely giving the boss a whip.

Management progressed from this to a form of collaboration and reason, where programs were explained to employees in an effort to enlist their support. This is the style in current use. It asks little of the employees except to try to understand as management explains its goals, and then help get the job done.

But what we find evolving today is the nondirective approach which we hope will lead to involvement in the enterprise and a commitment on the part of everyone to see that it succeeds. This is the desirable style for the future. Why? Because good people do not have to work for us anymore, and they know it. We can keep all of the mediocre folks we want, but the good ones are going to achieve self-fulfillment or they are going to leave.

The attrition rate in banks among people training for management in the last decade has been astounding. Banking blamed it on the mobility of the young people and their lack of desire to stick it out. I am confident, though, that a great deal of the fault lay with an industry which was complacent and insensitive to the real needs of its employees. We're improving, but we need to study this problem continually for two good reasons:

1. We must glean future management personnel from among the bright young people.

2. We must counter the threat of unionization from nonmanagement personnel through (a) job security, (b) salaries, (c) supervisors, (d) grievance procedures.

How do you evaluate a good manager or a good president today? The real measure is what is happening to the people who report to him. In what positions does he have them, compared to where they need to be? Does he have a team of managers that is performing and that knows its responsibilities?

Another vital consideration in measuring an executive is how well he carries out his appraisal procedure for subordinates. Is he committed enough to good management to have the discipline both to appraise and to be appraised?

Professional management works, and in its simplest form involves only three simple steps. First, get the square pegs in the square holes and the round pegs in the round holes. Put people where they are suited to work. Second, allow them to set goals for themselves which are meaningful to them, and third, religiously and personally review their progress in relation to these goals—and only these goals.

Here are some distinctions between the real professional manager and the other guy. The pro thinks before he acts and manages change. The other guy reacts and is always at the mercy of events.

The pro has a plan. He knows in advance what he wants to do, how he wants to do it, and when. The other guy solves crises. Take my advice and never reward the solving of crises. You will only perpetuate them.

The pro compares what he does to a predetermined plan, while the other guy compares results to past performance because that is easier.

The pro has a program of continual self-review, analysis, and correction. The other guy's program involves continual self-satisfaction.

It all comes down to the fact that the pro makes things happen.

The professional manager does not issue all orders, make all decisions, or solve all of the problems; neither does he permit his subordinate managers to do so. Good people want to become involved and participate in the management process. They can't work for a man who tries to harness all of the power. Mark Twain said, "Keep away from people who try to belittle your ambitions. Small people always do that, but the really great make you feel that you, too, can become great."

Management may be defined not as the direction of things but as the development of people. An organization chart for a bank has two important purposes. It tells who manages whom, and equally important, who does not manage whom. What I mean is that the executive vice-president should not become directly involved with the problems of the draft teller, for in doing so he completely relieves the cashier or some other subordinate manager of his responsibility for the teller's performance.

The management team in your bank must understand its responsibilities. Good people want their own ball park to play in, regardless of its size, and they want the boss to stay out unless he is invited. They also want their contributions to the big picture used—their knowledge, their special skills. But in fairness to the team, those who are not good managers must be replaced. There are three types of people: those who make things happen, those who watch things happen, and those who don't know what's happening. The president should be looking for those managers who make things happen, and should give them plenty of room to grow. He should also have a constructive weeding-out process for those who don't fit. It is sometimes too easy to rationalize keeping a dud around who will eventually become a morale problem.

All meaningful development is self-development, and we must never view our people as being static, for they are always in process. Self-fulfillment can be achieved only under a manager who says to his subordinate, "Here's where you are, here's where you need to be, and I want to help you." The managers you need offer to their subordinates opportunity, guidance, assistance, and incentive while these subordinates develop themselves.

Is there the proper management mix in the bank? Are there seniors who can offer experience and judgment, who can remember the bad days and help guide the younger managers away from too liberal an approach? Are there junior managers who are being given decisions to make?

As for the proper age mix of management, the acceptable age of any manager is that age from which he can think into the future. When he begins to lose this ability, his usefulness as a manager is reduced proportionately. I have heard that the fellow who says he is too old to learn probably always was.

The practical considerations of retirement have to be faced. In studying the policy, consideration should be given to the willingness of managers and directors to come to grips with change and to make the necessary adjustments in the present to insure a profitable future. Also to be considered is the creation of opportunities for young people to move up and be heard. No matter what the policy is regarding retirement, make it specific and have it written down for both officers and directors. And don't compromise it; morale will be ruined.

The proper practice of management requires participative supervision, for change imposed is change opposed. Participation on the part of subordinates leads to understanding, results in contribution, and achieves commitment on the part of the people in the organization. It requires open communication between manager and subordinate in which both keep their impulses focused on the task to be performed. In this type of environment, the manager can never relinquish his position as boss. The boss never takes a vote, for he cannot abdicate his responsibility to make decisions.

This is not self-management. It focuses on the task, and not on authority or friendship. It says to the subordinate, "I'll listen to anything you have to say, and I'll not cut you up if you disagree with me. I have my own hostilities which I can vent on my boss or my board. But once we've had our confrontation, I must fulfill my responsibility and make a decision. Then you should carry it out as if it were your own idea. And if you don't, or if you can't do it well, you've got to go."

A discussion of human resource management isn't complete today without consideration being given to the transition in organization form that we are experiencing in order better to relate the goals of the organization with the personal goals of its people. A psychologist named Maslow proposed that the physiological requirements of people must be met first, followed in order by safety, love, self-esteem, and finally self-actualization. And since most of the people who work for us in this affluent age have the first three, it is the challenge of the organization to provide for its people the self-esteem and self-actualization they seek in return for increased productivity.

We find many values in transition today as our organizations adjust to their people's needs, and here are some that we can recognize:

We are moving away from the idea that man is bad toward the recognition that he is basically good, away from negative evaluation of people toward confirmation of them as individuals, away from the view of man as fixed toward one of his being continually in process, away from maskmanship and game-playing toward authentic behavior, away from the use of power to preserve status toward its use for organizationally relevant purposes, away from distrusting people toward trusting them, away from avoiding facing facts toward appropriate confrontation, and finally away from an emphasis on competition toward an emphasis on collaboration.

I think the growth of our banks is keyed to our success in continuing this transition. Directors must face the basic requirement of providing their organization not with managers in name only who have been put there by the power structure, but with managers who are leaders.

These managers will be recognized as leaders only if they have clear objectives and plans for their achievement. They must let their people know the objectives and plans, and they must always have a mind open to their subordinates' ideas. The objectives must be good and the standards high, for subordinates like a good outfit.

The effective leader must have three types of competence—one, technical, which may be borrowed, and two, managerial and interpersonal, which cannot be borrowed. The effective leader invites engagement and confrontation. He lets his subordinates argue. He gets emotionally involved with the task and not with the people. He has concern for his subordinates and builds his relationship with them on trust.

Leaders have a special way of describing the job to be done, requiring that it be done well, but never letting people feel alone or having them grope for a reason to contribute. Our employees must be able to relate in a meaningful way to our goals and our overall approach to the customer, the prospect, and the community. It is not enough simply to say, "Our goal is profit."

This brings me to a final point—one which should concern all directors. That is the need to attract suitable future leaders. John Gardner wrote that a high proportion of the college population is receiving what amounts to an antileadership vaccine. He suggests that while the image students associate with the scholar, the scientist, and the professional man is one of dedication, honesty, and disinterest in worldly ambitions, the image of the corporate leader is that of a status-seeker, a man whose values are plastic and easily compromised, a man whose only goal in life is a shallow, shabby thing called profit. Because of this image problem, it appears that more and more young talent is deciding that leadership in the community is associated with goals that are distasteful because they are not compatible with individual human goals.

These leaders are needed in banking, and the only way to overcome the developing credibility gap is to pursue the goals of banking organizations in ways that are believable in human terms, in ways that have meaning for our employees.

To paraphrase Mr. Gardner: The thing that makes a number of individuals a bank, rather than a crowd of people handling specialized, separated pieces of work, is the presence of shared attitudes, habits, and values; a shared conception of the enterprise of which they are a part; shared views of why it is worthwhile for the enterprise to continue and to flourish.

Directors and management personnel must be trained to help bring about a healthy kind of community within our banks. Good leaders help to define and articulate and pursue the values that are cherished most. In short, they offer moral leadership, and this is the key to proper management of human resources.

Resource management is in the final analysis a responsibility of a bank's management to see that the basic commodities—dollars and people—are wisely used to provide a desirable future for the institution. The board, as it represents the stockholders, really has this future in its hands as it sets the benchmarks for management's long- and short-range performance. And that, in short, is a big job.

P. J. MILLS

The Banker and Public Affairs

FROM THE DAYS of the framing of the Constitution of this country in 1787 to the present time, American businessmen and politicans alike have realized that a progressive expanding economy has to be the joint concern of private enterprise and government. Almost every moment in the life of every business is affected by what government does, and never more in the history of this country than today.

In today's world the banker, as a businessman, cannot afford to be unaware of and uninvolved in what goes on in the public sector. For far too long, bankers have been reluctant to take an interest in public affairs. Many have been far too concerned about the potential critics who would accuse them of meddling in politics. As one who was active in community and political affairs while serving as a vice-president of a bank, I would like to say that there is no need for such an attitude.

There are a number of reasons why bankers must and should involve themselves in both community and political processes. Not the least of these reasons is the basic tenet of democracy which says that every person has the right to speak out and take a position to protect and further his own interests. But, correlative to that, he also has a duty to do so. The founding fathers of this nation imposed that condition on society.

The policies and decisions of governmental bodies at all levels, from regulatory agencies to the Congress itself, vitally affect the operations of business in banking.

The particular attitude that now prevails in this country is indeed cynical and rigid, and as a matter of fact, just plain untrue. It is not inappropriate, as some traditionalists would say, for bankers to attempt to inject themselves into the policy-making processes of their community, of their state, and of their nation. There is no good reason for bankers to be reluctant to do this, for, after all, in what industry in America is government more involved than in banking?

It has been my observation that the banking industry has been one of the least organized, and in many cases the least aggressive, sectors in society in terms of explaining its needs to the policy-makers in government. Certainly, efforts have been made in some areas, but it is vital that bankers realize that the system can be responsive in many, many ways. It is also vital that they realize that the system will not come to them, that they must go to the system. As they say in the country, the squeaking wheel gets the grease.

Businessmen have an obligation to offer government at every level the benefit of their special knowledge and expertise. And where else but in banking do you find such diverse knowledge and expertise when it comes to an understanding of what makes this country's economy tick?

There is no reason why bankers and other businessmen should be silent and aloof while everyone else speaks out. Indeed, it has been my experience, as a legislator in the Louisiana House of Representatives, that lawmakers want and appreciate factual information and expert opinions from executives who have done their homework on complex legislative issues.

Private interest and public interest are sometimes, but not necessarily, opposed. Indeed, the fundamental theory of the American economic system is that in the long run the pursuit of numerous private interests will best serve the overall public interests.

Government officials are not omniscient, and often they are not able to discern clearly what is best for the public interest. Government makes many decisions in many areas, and many times bitter debate precedes and follows these decisions.

Does anyone dare to maintain that the government of this country has exhibited such supreme wisdom and foresight in all matters that we should entrust it with total control over all the rest of our choices? We should, I think, agree that government can often use a helping hand. And who is to supply it if we shun our right and our duty to take part in the policy-making process?

Some are discouraged by the bigness of government. This should not, however, be a factor. Big government is made up of many smaller units, each accessible in one way or another. The fact that government regulates a particular area of interest does not necessarily reduce the individual's potential for influence in that area.

Some controls exercised by private agencies have been known to be much more rigid and restrictive than state controls. In other words, the individual banker may be able to influence government much more than he could ever hope to influence certain parts of the private sector.

I'm not necessarily suggesting that banks, as institutions, should be directly involved with politics, but I am stating that bankers in the banking industry, and those who make it up, should use their great potential for mobilizing human resources to accomplish specific ends.

How this capacity will be used is one of the great challenges facing this industry today. To my way of thinking, banking has the potential to work for its own ends as well as for the well-being of society.

The question, specifically, is how fully and effectively the ability to organize and pursue goals can and will be used to increase the resources of the American banking industry and thus of society.

How, for instance, can this ability be used to reduce the burden of poverty in this country? How can it be used to enrich the quality of life of the American people? How can it be used to deal with problems of ecology in substandard housing, of urban decay and poor transportation, of diminishing raw materials? How can it be used to bring about a greater degree of equality of opportunity?

Banks are highly visible symbols of the United States economic system—all the more so since they have grown huge, have gone into more fields and have sought the business of consumers as well as that of giant corporations. Men schooled to weigh each loan application and each investment for its soundness and its return, men conditioned to measure subordinates by the color of their school ties, have had to learn some new rules of the game. A critical facet of the new banking is a growing awareness of its obligation to society.

Today bankers find themselves under acute pressure to make loans, not because they would yield the most, but because they are socially desirable, and to refuse loans to companies that pollute or make war materials, and to companies that practice outright discrimination. I'm not saying that they should follow this practice, but they are under pressure to do this by many people who use their banks to vote the shares held by their trust departments against management and for proposals backed by environmentalists and various minority groups. The pressure is stronger every day.

Similarly, bankers are under pressure to hire more blacks and minorities, and more women, and to promote them as rapidly as possible, considering them on the basis of their capability, not their sex or their race.

The solution for some may simply involve a change of attitude. But the most difficult of the problems confronting business today is not deciding whether it has an obligation to serve social needs, but rather determining how it may do so effectively. Confronting this challenge and dealing with it adequately is one of the most important tasks of business today. It is important for all of us, for society as well as for business.

Business will bear its responsibility to serve society primarily because such service is ethically right, and ultimately because it is legally necessary. Yet, as business struggles to find the best means of providing for social needs and of responding to the pressures brought upon it, it may find that the responses it devises serve not only special interests in society, but also business itself.

Socially responsible conduct may also be economically profitable. Consider, for example, the assembly line in America, a great industrial advance that was once regarded as socially progressive. It afforded a means of industrial efficiency that provided higher wages for the ordinary worker than economists had ever thought possible. It has been an important element in the productivity of this country.

Yet as the economy has increased its productivity and its capacity through technology, it has produced an increasingly affluent society in which workers are no longer satisfied merely to earn a comfortable living. Workmen are now demanding not only adequate wages, but also psychological fulfillment.

In reorganizing work patterns to meet these new demands, business may find new methods of productivity that are better adapted to contemporary conditions, more productive than the new technological environment, and thus more advantageous for everyone.

The chief executive of the Chase Manhattan Bank, a traditional citadel of capitalism, has said that business must begin devising incentive systems which will lead more private enterprises to serve public needs and at the same time make a profit. He said that businessmen have no choice but to become reformers themselves by making a conscious effort to adapt the market system to our rapidly changing social, political, and technological environment.

Whether or not you fully agree with all such ideas, I think you will agree that banks must adapt to this changing world of ours. And despite some stuffy talk that I hear now and then, the modern successful bank is one of the most change-oriented institutions of our society. If you don't believe it, just look around your own town and compare your bank and the new banks that have come in recently with what existed ten or fifteen years ago.

Banks are flexible because bankers realize that flexibility is directly related to competition and survival. In that regard, banks can sometimes be envisioned as instruments of change, not only in the economic field, but in the field of social advances as well.

Enlightened banks are also awakening to the need to relax some of the old restrictions on what activities their employees can engage in. They are recognizing the value of encouraging individuals with interest in public affairs. Who in the community in which you live knows that community better than do the people who work in your bank?

I was fortunate enough to work for a bank with this attitude. I spent four years in the Louisiana legislature, and I was given time off from the bank during the legislative sessions, and also in the interim, to serve on special committees in order to pursue the evasive but in my opinion extremely worthwhile goal of better government for the state in which I live.

Management at some other banks might not have been so encouraging, fearing that my political involvement might stir damaging controversy. In most cases, I think the premise of that argument is overrated. In fact, the most vigorous criticism I have ever heard directed at a bank was directed at those who did nothing.

In four years as a legislator, I experienced only one instance of a person who had a connection with our bank saying anything about a stand that I took on a particular issue; and when I got through talking to him, I changed his mind. And as one indication of my efforts to promote more businesslike government, I introduced in my first session as a member of the legislature an Idle Funds Investment Law. This didn't sit too well with a lot of my colleagues in the banking industry, but I wasn't elected to the legislature to represent just the banking community. I was elected to represent what was in the best interests of the State of Louisiana.

That little change in the law produced, in fiscal 1973, twenty million dollars of revenue for the state of Louisiana. And prior to its passage in 1970, the state of Louisiana realized a little over two and a half million dollars from that source.

An enlightened bank will have no unreasonable restrictions on what civic or political interests its employees may have. The uninhibited discussion of viewpoints, ideas, and facts is conducive to arriving at rational democratic decisions.

Bank management, in my opinion, can commit a grave sin by giving its employees the feeling that the expression of social or political ideas is frowned upon. Many people are unwilling to express ideas when they think they will suffer unfavorable consequences, and that, in my opinion, is what's wrong with this country today.

One of the characteristics of politics is that it is controversial; but without politics as we know it the government of this country cannot function. This automatically establishes the possibility of disagreement with ideas, and some people will avoid even accidental disagreement with management, fearing some sort of reprisal.

Management should, therefore, take active steps to let employees know that they should vote, that they should be registered to vote, that they should take part in civic affairs, and that their opinions will be respected, not attacked.

If employees think that political discussions and activities may have a harmful effect on their occupational success, they will feel stifled. A stifling atmosphere is precisely what is not needed today. Apathy is running away with this country.

In March, 1974, in Orleans Parish where I live, a very significant election was held for the renewal of certain taxes and for several other issues, one of which was the election of a senator to fill a vacancy in the state legislature. Only 20 percent of the qualified voters turned out to vote. In 1971, in the election for governor of Louisiana, almost one million of those qualified to vote stayed home; and this is not something that is peculiar to the state of Louisiana. It's a disease that infects the American public—a tendency to say, "Let someone else do it; just let me gripe about what happens."

No one should feel that political activity is futile. It is futile only when you don't get involved and when you don't take the trouble to vote. Individuals can make a difference. Participation can translate one's will into action. Never feel that there is no point in doing something, because we live in a democracy and, whether you believe it or not, all the political and governmental institutions in this country are responsive, in varying degrees, to the will of the people.

The reasons why these institutions sometimes appear unresponsive is that too few people try to get them to respond. It's a mistake to feel that the political destiny of this country is in the hands of some nebulous, unseen "somebody else." In a democratic society like ours, the people are the "somebody else."

There are no powerful anonymous forces making all the decisions in this country, in your community, or in the state in which you live. The people who make decisions for you and in your behalf have names, addresses, offices, and telephone numbers. They can know what you're thinking and what you feel ought to be done, at whatever level of government you are interested in, only if you let them know. And if you don't think that the people you elect to public office are responsive to your contacting them about a particular issue, just try them one time.

I believe the answer to the question of whether the banker can afford not to be involved in public affairs is patently clear. The banker can, should, and must become involved. It is his duty, not only to his employees and his shareholders, but to a much greater institution which makes it possible for his bank acually to exist, the United States of America.

PART THREE

Credit Administration

FRANK A. PLUMMER

Loan Policies

BEFORE REVIEWING the subject material of credit administration, it might be well to explore the political and economic environment of the banking industry in 1974, first as it relates to the whole industry, and then as it relates to the southern section of our nation.

Two significant changes in the financial world are no longer on the horizon—they have arrived!

Whether we enjoy it or not, it is obvious that the gyrations of the money market in recent years have cast fear into the hearts of Congress concerning the plight of the savings and loan institutions, to such an extent that we will see a wave of legislation permitting savings and loans most of the prerogatives formerly reserved to commercial banking. This in turn will mean more branching by city savings and loans into smaller communities, which means more competition. We will also see more competition from areas such as credit unions, finance companies, and insurance companies for business we formerly considered our private domain.

There is a second significant change within our own industry: the coming of age of the registered multibank holding company. At the present time holding companies control approximately 66 percent of the nation's deposits. By 1980 I predict they will control 90 percent. Without probing this subject in depth, let me say quickly that it means more competition within our industry.

There is one other significant economic development: the energy crunch. What does this mean to banking? In the next few years, as we seek energy independence, billions of dollars will be required for development. Also, I believe that we will see a flood of new industry locating in our section of the country, the south, to be near our type of energy and for other reasons. All of these changes mean two things:

fierce competition and more opportunity than we have ever enjoyed.

As bank directors, we are responsible for loan policy. How does it relate?

For the last several months I have been studying loan policy in our own bank and in other commercial banks. The traditional format, in my opinion, will not survive the competition ahead of us. We must change policy from a negative stance to a positive posture. After a determination of the types of loans you wish to make, you couch policy in such terms as: this bank is anxious to make agricultural loans; this bank will cultivate the loans of professional men and women in medical and related fields; this bank will give thrust to real estate construction loans and permanent mortgages in the twenty-five-year range.

No longer can we write policy in terms that leave the young lending officer in fear and trembling that he or she will break a taboo. This mental atitude will not stand the heat of competition.

Is an aggressive, positive loan policy inconsistent with sound loan administration? No indeed! A well-written loan policy will have annexes: an annex for mortgage loans, an annex for consumer loans, etc. In these annexes you outline proper procedures and subtly draw the perimeters around certain types of lending. These guidelines should eliminate careless mistakes and discipline judgment. In the main body, however, you have given direction to your program.

Now, as we draft our loan policy for "X" bank, what are some questions that we as directors should answer? Your bank might have an unusual twist, but normally I think loan policy has to have a minimal gutty list of prescriptions. These include: (1) geographical limits to the lending function, (2) allocation of loans among functions, (3) consumer credit policy and mortgage loan policy, (4) the loan to deposit ratio to be sustained, (5) interest rate schedules applicable under various conditions, (6) loan limits for officers and committees, (7) procedures for supervising lines of credit, (8) participation procedures, and (9) the process and timing of loan review.

By these or similar prescriptions, what have we accomplished?

1. We have eliminated confusion, for ourselves and the customer. All officers have the same loan policy.

2. As directors we are directing.

3. We have eliminated "looking over the shoulder" of the officer by prescribing standard policy.

Now, as directors can we relax? *Not quite!* We are in the position of "Bear" Bryant when he has a good "game plan," but finds the other coach has better players. (This doesn't happen very often.)

No, as directors operating through your executive officer, you are responsible for putting good loan officers on the firing line. It is like any business. You *recruit* good people. You have a continuing training program, and then you make certain that you have a good program of compensation and motivation so that you retain the good ones.

There is one other area of personnel important to a successful loan program: the composition of the directors' loan committee. Be sure that you have all round pegs in round holes. For example, I like automobile dealers on a loan committee to help on consumer credit policies; I like contractors to help with their knowledge of real estate developers.

The point I am making is that being the largest stockholder or the oldest member of the board does not necessarily qualify you for this particular committee.

I think we are making progress with our loan administration. We have taken a look at our community and our bank and decided what constructive program we want to improve the bank and the community and to use our depositors' funds in a constructive, sound way. We then adopted loan policies and put them in writing. We then recruited a good team to implement the policies.

Is there any ingredient lacking? You bet! A very important ingredient: loan review.

Bank directors are responsible for their bank's having a loan review program. Why? Not, certainly, to lock the door after the horse is stolen. It should be a continuing program to prevent losses and to make certain you are doing the job. When you have such a program:

1. You have a chance to find out whether lending officers are adhering to policy.
2. You detect trouble while you can take corrective action.
3. You catch the sleepers: no prepayment program, low interest rates, etc.
4. You catch loans without credit files, without collateral, without insurance.
5. You evaluate the officers. Who has the volume? Who has too many losses? Who never has a loss? (Fire both of them!)

Every bank can tailor a review program to its own needs. In our bank we copy the FBI. Instead of the *ten most wanted* we have the *twenty most sorry*—most sorry loans in the bank. We start with a committee of junior officers; from that committee to the loan committee, and then to my desk. I then review three loans with the most exposure with directors each month.

For a moment let us suppose each one of us is on the loan review committee and we are looking at the loans. What tests can we apply? Well, here are five questions which will smoke out a lot of trouble:

1. What is the purpose?
2. With whom are we doing business?
3. What is the repayment program?
4. What and where is the cushion?
5. Does it all make sense?

If my directors knew how easy it was to loan money, they would cut my salary.

CHESTER A. RUDE

Sound Credit Administration and the Director

THE FUNCTION of commercial banking as we know it in this country is to act as a reservoir for surplus funds and, in turn, to lend a safe portion of these funds to those who have a constructive need for credit. Deposits are the raw material with which we work. These deposits do not belong to us; they belong to the depositors. It is important to keep reminding ourselves of this fact.

As trustees for these deposits, we have a very special responsibility to the area we serve. The way in which we handle these funds will largely determine whether we are laying a sound foundation or creating future problems for the borrower, ourselves, and the economy. If we withhold credit unwisely, business suffers and so do the people in our respective communities. If we extend credit too freely, overexpansion takes place and ultimately the economy suffers. Also, banks are quasi-public institutions because we have a franchise to create deposit currency.

Because of this trustee relationship, we have to operate under very special laws and supervision. A study of the history of commercial banking will indicate why our banking laws are what they are and why they are needed. It shows the reason why many new laws and regulations have been necessary, and it likewise shows that in spite of very special laws it is impossible to legislate judgment. That is why it disturbs me to hear of leverage for stockholders in the form of debentures, preferred stock, etc.

It should be emphasized repeatedly that both statutory and common law have placed the responsibility for the management of banks—whether it involves the lending function or the investment function—on the members of the bank's board of directors.

How can the directors know that "sound credit administration" is being followed? We shouldn't expect a director to have the knowledge or the time to be an experienced loan officer, or to pass on individual loan applications. Neither can we expect him to devote the time required to know the intimate details of every loan. It must inevitably mean a delegation of authority and responsibility, based on his judgment of the quality of management.

It should be the desire of good management to devise ways of keeping directors thoroughly informed of all phases of the bank's operations and policies. The directors, on the other hand, should not be involved in the function of management. They should hold management responsible for results.

The director should know the loan policy and be supplied with sufficient information to enable him to determine the quality of the loan portfolio. The volume of loans and their size will dictate the best procedure.

Directors and Committees

All loans must be approved by the directors. As a matter of time, only the large loans and commitments can actually be studied at a board meeting. The board should therefore designate certain committees to study and approve smaller loans. These committees can be designated as the executive committee or loan committee of the board.

All directors should, in time, serve as revolving members on these committees and faithfully attend meetings. It is, of course, recognized that a large loan for a bank may be $50,000, $500,000, or $1,000,000, depending upon the bank.

The essential facts about each loan set out in stencil form for each director should be approximately as follows:

Name
Line of Business
Current Assets
Current Liabilities
Working Capital
Net Worth
Sales
Earnings
Balances
Amount of Loan—Expiration Date—Rate
Loan—Secured or Unsecured—Special Terms

As businessmen, you can pretty well judge the quality of a loan from the information above the last two lines.

The directors' examining committee should have permanent, as well as revolving, members of the board. In this way, each board member will become familiar with loan policy and how it is being carried out. This complete review of all loans at least twice a year should give the director a complete understanding of the quality of the loan portfolio. It is especially important that each loan officer appear before this committee to answer any questions about the loans he is handling. One of the major benefits in having loan officers appear before the examining committee is the opportunity for directors to evaluate the competence of each officer. All problem loans should be discussed and studied as to future collectibility or loss. The trend of criticized items, the program for eliminating them, will give the director a feel of whether management is carrying out sound loan policy.

Loan Policy

The loan policy of each individual bank must take into consideration the bank's capital funds in relation to deposits, the character of its deposits, and the diversification of its deposits and loans.

One-industry or one-crop areas call for a much more conservative loan policy than areas with a vast diversification in agriculture and industry. This same reasoning should apply in determining the percentage of risk assets to capital.

A loan policy for the individual bank should cover, but not be limited to, a general idea of the needs for commercial, agricultural, real estate, consumer, and special industry types of credit. It might include term loans, lease transactions, and commodity loans. The deposit structure, the trend of deposits, and the investment account will have a bearing on the planning of the loan program.

How should we determine the amount of loans desirable for each bank? With the tremendous increase in deposits caused by deficit financing, a major war, and inflation, the percentage of loans to deposits is only a partial guide.

I think it is always unwise to make rules as to what percentage of deposits should be in loans, or how many dollars of capital there should be for a given number of dollars of loans. If your loans exceed the average of loans to deposits for banking as a whole in your area, perhaps you are too liberal with your loan terms. If the ratio of loans to capital is likewise higher than the average, there is reason to scrutinize your loan portfolio. It might show a fine earning record on capital, but it might also mean an investment in risk assets which is out of proportion, thereby bringing about a risk to future dividends and possibly some capital.

The guideline questions on lending policy for national bank directors formulated by the Comptroller of the Currency are as follows:

1. Has the Board of Directors or its designated Committee formulatd a program of sound lending policies?
2. Does over-all lending policy reflect an awareness by the bank of its responsibility in meeting the legitimate credit needs of the community?
3. Is there diversification in its loan portfolio?
4. Is the necessity for current, complete, and reliable credit information recognized by management?
5. Has the bank established a realistic repayment program at the inception of all loans?
6. Is the repayment program enforced?
7. Is there a program for periodic review, inspection, or administration?
8. Is a salvage policy for charged-off loans pursued energetically?

Corporate treasurers are flattered by the bank which grants its legal loan limit, and officers of banks are proud to show their confidence in a company that gives them their legal limit. This is questionable loan policy. For the protection of the company they represent, corporation treasurers should rarely accept legal loan limits. And as a matter of good loan policy, a bank should establish a "house limit" which is less than the legal limit.

If a company needs more credit than the house limit, they should seek additional banking connections. This may be difficult, even when conditions are good. If conditions are bad, and the borrower's credit is strained, the legal limit bank can do nothing, even though it should, to protect itself; and it is a certainty that new bank lines are not going to be granted to bail out a competitor.

Importance of Facts

Intelligent loaning of money means getting the facts—all the facts. Then and only then will intelligent judgment be used. To assemble those facts adequate credit files should be maintained and any officer in the bank or the director or examiner should be able to appraise the quality of the loan from the facts in the credit file.

The test of a good loan policy should be: (1) Is it a good asset for the bank? (2) Is it good for the borrower? (3) Is it good for the economy of the area the bank serves?

When a banker makes loans solely because they are safe, or to add to his earnings, without regard to the effect on the borrower and the community, he is endangering his bank and the economy of his area.

Good loan policy is not trying to see how much money can be loaned. Good loan policy is trying to see how wisely money can be loaned. Making credit too easy, spreading it around too far, must inevitably create problems for our customers and our banks.

ROY D. HARTMANN

Credit Administration

THE LOAN OFFICER who really knows the company he is dealing with and the industry of which that company is part can be of tremendous importance to and have an impact on his customer. The importance of the subject of credit can easily be translated into its impact on the bank itself, with total loans equaling 60 percent of total assets of a bank and contributing two-thirds of a bank's gross income.

I would like to discuss the subject of credit as your credit administrator, remembering that as an administrator my primary charge is to implement policy.

Whereas I should not be dependent upon you to make my day-to-day line decisions for me, I am absolutely dependent upon you to set the overall policy giving me the direction I need to do my job. When talking about policy itself, consider:

1. Loan policy should be in writing (for consistency, protection).

2. Loan policy should blend with and be consistent with all other stated bank policies. As we talk about such things as asset management, liability management, personnel policies, marketing policies, etc., it is clear that the interrelations of all of these together give a line officer the total direction that he needs and make him confident of having his own performance measured in terms of the overall results.

3. Loan policy, like every other policy, must be responsive to ever changing conditions and therefore must be reassessed and revised regularly.

A loan policy structured toward a loan/deposit ratio is important, but I feel that there is much more need for a policy that responds to a planned percentage contribution of loans by type. This will give the administrator an overall picture of the kind (commercial, real estate, consumer; plus industries by type) of loan portfolio he is to build.

Realizing the varying maturities of a ninety-day note commercial loan, a five-year term loan, a thirty-year real estate loan, a three-year consumer loan, and a revolving consumer credit line, this type of asset management will help significantly to make overall liquidity of the portfolio more manageable. The credit administrator, through effective profit planning, can set priorities and objectives designed to arrive at the percentage of composition by loan kind that you have established.

In the last ten years, we have seen commercial banks shift in total liabilities from a 70 percent demand and 30 percent time position to a 45 percent demand deposit and 55 percent time deposit posture. This change has had and will have significant impact on future policy decisions as to the percentage of makeup of loans by kind and maturity. The future trend toward more and more time funds is apparent. A bank's capability to buy funds in the marketplace and match against loan investments and maturities is bringing us closer to liability management as a way of life. The changing liability composition of banks to the interest paid time deposits is changing the objectives of banks and their willingness to make aggressively the longer maturity real estate and commercial term loans. We also see a significant trend of deposit ownership in banks from the large companies to the consumer. This impacts heavily on our loan policy decisions and allocation of loanable funds.

The package concept of tying together all aspects of a consumer's financial borrowing needs is a key factor in the bank's deposit growth, and strategically it has the potential of holding the consumer to the same bank much longer. It also follows that the bank should try to get the individual as a customer when he is young.

The geographic area in which we are to make loans should be very clearly defined. I am sure we would all agree that when we take deposit money out of our service area, we have a responsibility to put it back on an economically sound basis. That, of course, cannot include a license to make bad loans, but should include a willingness to set a credit policy that is first and foremost responsive to those needs. As a bank, we should know our own service area best and should be capable of judging the quality of loans most effectively. With that judgment made, allocation of lendable funds should be established via a policy of in/out participations with other banks, loans outside of a bank's own service area, or internationally if large enough. It should be recognized that when we go outside of our service area we often must deal with more unknowns that can lead to more difficult credit decisions.

The allocation of authority for line lending officers is a must in any credit administration plan. Loan officers prefer dollar lending limits because they eliminate doubts and have a definite tendency to increase their self-confidence. That self-confidence also seems to pass itself on to their customers. I would recommend that you delegate authority limits within the bank at the various line levels to as high a dollar amount as you comfortably can. Lending officers are cautious and seldom abuse authority. This definitely speeds up the decision-making process. This approach allows the loan committee to become more of a review committee, concerned more with adherence to policy and proper credit concepts requiring actual approval of the very large credits only. One key to the permitting of maximum lending authority limits may be found in a good procedure for supporting in writing the loan made. (Although the officer may have committed the loan, he still would have accountability for supporting his decision.) The written presentation required must define the purpose of the loan, the source of repayment, a financial statement, spread sheets and analysis of same, description of collateral, if any, and any miscellaneous comments that help to explain the nature of the company's business, its management, and its future prospects. In other words, the basic credit issues are identified and related to the transaction. A technique that can add flexibility to the authority process is the use of approved lines of credit, generally of a one-year duration. This type of arrangement permits the borrower to borrow up to this sum on a revolving basis. A line commitment of this nature can be either internal (customer not aware of the line) or firm (line committed to the customer).

In relating to the purpose of a commercial loan, I think it is important to differentiate as to whether the credit itself is a working capital loan or a term loan in nature. We often think of a working capital loan as that type of credit extended for relatively short periods of time (less than one year) and self-liquidating in nature, the repayment then coming from the ultimate reduction of the working asset. A working capital loan made seasonally to increase inventory for a relatively short period of time and then repaid from the reduction of the inventory level to a normal level would be an example of this type of credit. When considering a term loan, we normally think of a credit extended for a purpose such as a fixed asset acquisition, the repayment of which normally would come from future cash flow earnings of the business, generally liquidating in installments over a long duration (in excess of one year). Therefore, the purpose of the loan and its source of repayment must be sufficiently identifiable to establish capacities to handle the transaction.

When considering a commercial loan it is also, in my opinion, a good practice to establish a secondary source of repayment should the primary source referred to not materialize as planned.

The subject of delegation of authority leads into that of our joint responsibilities for the recruitment, training, and retention of capable lending officers. With the advent of more complex and specialized kinds of commercial lending, such as interim finance, commercial lease financing, international finance, etc., there is the need either to have this type of expertise available or to avoid the field. Be aware of a continuous capability of your bank for training lending officers. Internal credit workshops, external seminars, banking schools, large correspondent banks, all can help in the training process. Training a young loan officer well, giving him hefty authority and responsibility, and rewarding him for his efforts—this is the best combination I know of to retain him in your bank.

A loan approval system must be combined with a system to review those credits extended in the past that have deteriorated in quality to a point where the loan committee should have monthly visibility. I would suggest that a candidate for this review should be either (1) a loan currently classified by the National Bank Examiners; (2) a loan that in the opinion of the lending officer or the loan committee bears a greater than normal risk; or (3) a loan that is thirty days delinquent. (The minimum dollar amount for the loans reviewed will vary with the size of your bank.)

The entire review and approval system presumes the existence of an efficient credit department where credit files and credit analysis can be prepared effectively to support the loan officer. This is the heart of the entire credit administration process. An efficient credit department can develop facts that are both timely and accurate, permitting more correct credit decisions.

The last major area of policy that I would like to touch on is that of pricing. Interest rate schedules should be a part of the credit administration process. Interest rates should be responsive to:

1. Competition.

2. Risk.

3. Cost of handling the loan. (For example, to follow an accounts receivable secured loan can cost several hours of work monthly.)

4. Maturity of loan. (Loan committed over one year should bring a slight premium.)

5. Gross yield (reflective of the total yield of a loan after considering total costs of handling all services performed for the customer).

6. Fees for commitments.

There are, of course, degrees of risk or lengths of maturity which mark the limits of what commercial banks can and should assure. Considering the nature of our liquidity needs and our responsibility to our depositors, stockholders, etc., these degrees must be identified and maintained. Inasmuch as we have an objective of helping to see that a customer's credit needs are fulfilled, it is to our advantage to be well aware of external alternate sources of financing and their capabilities so that in those situations that we cannot handle, at least at the moment, we can aid our customers by giving them the best possible advice.

In the future the computer can have, and I believe will have, much more capability to assist us, from the point of view of credit administration. Management information that relates to loans in the bank's portfolio by classification, maturity, industry, marketing potential, etc., can be of tremendous assistance to us in the management of the lending function. Also, total customer profitability, profitability by kinds of loans (consumer, real estate, commercial), will enable us in our planning process to make management decisions as to our priorities in business development emphasis and will help us plan and project our future objectives.

In the future, more kinds of loans made may well involve direct leasing, have more revolving credit for individuals, more real estate and other longer term loans, and more commercial loans secured by such security as accounts receivable, etc., to give more total flexibility to the lending function.

The loan demand will probably expand at a rate greater than normal deposit growth, forcing banks more and more to buy funds in other marketplaces. As this occurs, the interrelationship of changing loan policies responsive to a projected changing asset and liability structure of banks will be a very substantial challenge to each of us.

Specimen of a Statement of Lending Policies

The officers of this bank, in making loans, shall be guided by the following memorandum:

1. The management of the bank believes that sound loans are a desirable and profitable means of employing funds available for investment. Authorized bank employees are expected to make, and seek to develop, all of the sound loans that the resources of the bank permit and that opportunity affords. In the allocation of resources available for loans, primary consideration shall be given to existing or potential customers with economic interests in the Dayton area.

2. The Board of Directors realizes that the lending of money by the bank necessarily includes reasonable business risks. Some losses are to be expected in the lending program, and it is the policy of the Board of Directors to maintain a reserve for future loan losses as large as is allowed by pertinent banking and tax laws. Any officer may request of the Senior Loan Officer that a loan be charged off, but such credits shall be reduced to judgement on or before the decision to charge off when such action is consistent with good banking practice. It shall be the responsibility of the officers who approved the credits to continue to follow their loans after charge-off proceedings.

3. The administration of the bank's lending activities will be supervised by the Senior Loan Officer of the bank, and he shall follow the policies set forth in this resolution. The Senior Loan Officer shall seek the advice and counsel of the Executive Committee of the Board of Directors when in doubt as to credit decisions or questions involving the interpretation or application of loan policies.

4. All loans in excess of the limits herinafter provided for the various lending officers, and not to exceed the legal limit of the bank, shall be approved prior to consummation by one of the following:

A. The Executive Committee of the Board of Directors, or

B. An officer whose authorized limit is great enough to allow his individual approval of the loan, and/or

C. The Officers Loan Committee, which shall have the combined authority of all officers appointed thereto, the members and chairman of which shall be designated by the Executive Committee, ratified by the Board of Directors.

5. All loans shall be reported to the Executive Committee following disbursement and, in addition, loans and credit lines of $__________ and over, not specifically approved by the Executive Committee, shall be reported to the Executive Committee at its next meeting following such approval. Any loan to an individual or company which would place the total credit extended to a related group of individuals and/or companies in excess of the bank's legal lending limit must receive approval of the Executive Committee prior to disbursement.

6. The members and responsibilities of the Officers Loan Committee are set forth in Exhibit A which is attached hereto. The Executive Committee of the Board of Directors shall review these responsibilities no less than one time during each calendar year and the Executive Committee is authorized to make such changes in the Loan Committee and its responsibilities as it may consider prudent.

7. The lending representatives of the bank shall have the authority up to the amount as is indicated by their names, without the approval of any committee, provided such loans are in accordance with the policies and principals herein expressed. It is intended that the total liabilities of a borrower to the bank, including real estate, installment, and commercial loans, are not to exceed the authority of the lending representative approving the loan.

8. The Chief Executive Officer of the bank may, without specific authorization of the Board of Directors, grant lending authority of not more than $__________ to officers and/or employees. Such action must be reported to the Executive Committee at its next meeting and recorded in the minutes.

9. Loans of the following types are considered desirable by this bank. Each loan must meet the tests of a prudent loan:

A. Unsecured loans to business concerns and individuals on a short term basis, supported by a satisfactory balance sheet and earnings statement, usually for a term not to exceed 90 days, and

B. Loans to business concerns and individuals secured by a

security interest in marketable equipment, such loans to be amortized over a period of time generally not to exceed 36 months, and

C. Loans to companies against assignment of accounts receivable. Loans against assigned accounts receivable shall be supervised by an officer of the bank appointed by the Officers Loan Committee, and procedures for servicing the loan must be approved in advance by the Officers Loan Committee.

D. Loans collaterally secured by marketable bonds, and

E. Loans collaterally secured by securities listed on a recognized stock exchange; such loans must comply in *all respects* with regulation U of the Federal Reserve System.

F. Loans collaterally secured by unlisted securities which are readily marketable in the "over the counter" market, and

G. Loans against the cash surrender value of life insurance, such loans not to exceed the cash surrender value plus the accumulated dividends, and

H. Loans secured by the assignment of savings accounts in the bank, or other banks, or secured by savings accounts or share accounts of federally insured savings and loan associations, and

I. Loans under $__________ in amount secured by first liens on improved business or residential properties, such loans to qualify as follows:

1. Real Estate loans shall be in the form of an obligation secured by a first mortgage, and
2. Real Estate loans shall generally not exceed, in amount, _____% of the appraised value of the real estate offered as security, and
3. Real Estate loans shall generally not exceed a term of _____ years, amortized in equal installment payments, and
4. Real Estate appraisals upon which mortgage loans are based shall be made by appraisers who are approved by the Executive Committee.

J. Real Estate loans, in excess of $__________, governed by the principals as set forth in Section I, above, and approved in advance by the Executive Committee.

K. Installment loans, governed by Exhibit B of this "Statement of Lending Policies."

L. Commodity loans secured by warehouse receipts in bonded warehouses or by field warehouse receipts.

It should be recognized by each lending representative of the bank that it is to the advantage of the borrower and to the bank that each loan have a program of repayment, agreed upon at the time the loan is made.

It is evident that certain loans—due to the nature of supporting collateral—may, in reality, be less liquid than others. All loans, excluding real estate loans, shall be reviewed at least each quarter by the lending representative who initiated the loan, and when changes in the economy, the securities market, or the commodities market warrant, loans shall be reviewed more often.

All loans shall have an ample margin of safety between the advance and the current market value of the collateral. When insurance on the collateral or on the life of the borrower is warranted, it shall be obtained and periodically reviewed by the officer initiating the loan.

10. Loans of the following types are not considered desirable loans for the purposes of the bank. Such loans will ordinarily be declined unless they are specifically approved by the Officers Loan Committee or the Executive Committee of the Board of Directors for reasons which appear to justify an exception to the bank's general policy:

A. Capital loans to a business enterprise where the loan cannot be repaid within a reasonable period except by borrowing elsewhere or by liquidating the business.

B. Loans to a new enterprise if the repayment of the loan is dependent upon the profitable operation of the enterprise.

C. Loans to parties whose integrity or honesty is questionable.

D. Real Estate mortgage loans secured by property out of the bank's recognized trade area.

E. Construction mortgage loans, except in cases where the building is being supervised by an architect and/or a contractor having financial responsibility and where the borrower has produced a satisfactory take out commitment.

F. Loans to be paid from the proceeds of the settlement of an estate, unless these loans are fully collateralized or guaranteed by the estate and approved by bank counsel.

G. Loans secured by stock in a closed corporation which has no ready market.

H. Loans for the purpose of enabling the borrower to speculate on the future market of securities or commodities.

11. A written application must be prepared for all loans, in order

that the bank will have a written record of the representation upon which the loan was based and the agreed upon term of repayment.

12. Interest rates shall be in accordance with the schedule adopted by the Officers Loan Committee. The Officers Loan Committee shall review the interest rate schedule when deemed appropriate and shall make required changes.

13. All unsecured loans in excess of $1,000 must be supported by a current financial statement. Such financial statements shall contain sufficient information to support the loan, shall be signed by the borrower, or shall be certified by an acceptable independent public or certified public accountant to the extent determined by the Officers Loan Committee and/or the approving loan officer. Whenever possible fiscal statements are to be supplemented by interim statements and other financial information.

14. It shall be the duty of the credit manager to see that an appropriate memorandum for the credit file is prepared on each loan. The memorandum shall recite the circumstance under which the loan was made, the factors which justify it, and the borrower's plan of repayment.

15. Description and classification of collateral. (Note: The state of the economy and the susceptibility of the stock market to change may make the following advances imprudent. Each member of the lending staff shall take the full responsibility for appraising the original and continuing advisability of certain percentage advances against the following types of collateral. The following percentage advances are subject to change by the Executive Committee.)

Description and Classification of Collateral

CLASS A

1. U. S. Government securities (____% of market).
2. Securities of Federal Agencies (____% of market).
3. Stocks listed on New York Stock Exchange or American Stock Exchange (____% of market).
4. Municipal bonds rated by Moody's "A" or better (____% of market).
5. Cash surrender value of life insurance (full cash surrender value including accrued dividends).
6. Savings accounts in our bank (____% of amount on deposit).

CLASS B

1. Stocks listed on other security exchanges (____% of market).
2. Other bonds rated by Moody's or listed on a security exchange, or quoted in the Wall Street Journal (____% of market).
3. Mutual funds (____% of market).
4. Stocks quoted over the counter (____% of market).
5. Savings accounts of other banks, or share accounts of insured building and loans (____% of account).
6. F.H.A. Title I—Maximum to any one borrower (including spouse) limited by law.

CLASS C

1. Chattel mortgage and/or security agreement with appropriate filings.
2. Assigned accounts receivable.
3. Warehouse receipts on marketable commodities.
4. Unquoted stocks.
5. Real estate mortgages.
6. All other collateral.

Exhibit "A"

OFFICERS LOAN COMMITTEE

1. The Committee shall consist of the following members:

________________________, Chairman
________________________, Vice Chairman
____
____

The Chief Executive Officer of the bank shall be Chairman of the Committee and the Senior Lending Officer shall serve as Vice Chairman. Two members of the Committee shall constitute a quorum, and one of the two members shall act as Chairman in the absence of the Chief Executive Officer and the Senior Lending Officer.

2. All commercial loans and approvals of credit shall be reviewed or approved by the Committee. The Officers Loan Committee shall meet at least three times each week.

3. The authority of the Committee shall be equal to the combined authorities of the members in attendance.

4. Loans and credits of $____________ or more should, whenever

practicable, be made or committed only after approval of the Executive Committee.

5. The Credit Manager or his appointed representative will act as Secretary of the Committee and will be responsible for arranging the flow of material to meetings. Officers wishing to present matters to the Committee should so notify the Credit Department in advance.

Exhibit "B"

INSTALLMENT LOANS

It is the purpose of this exhibit to establish a uniform and proved approach to installment lending. The following comments and point evaluations will offer guidance and set standards for the granting of such credit. All consumer loans *MUST* be evaluated according to the point system currently in use and wherever possible the signatures of both husband and wife should be obtained. Any loan made where the total points indicate excessive risk must be fully justified *in writing* at the time the loan is made. All installment loans made which do not conform to both the bank's "Statement of Lending Policies" and this Exhibit "B" shall be reviewed by the officer in charge of installment loans. If the loan does not conform, the member of the lending staff approving the loan shall so indicate on the application.

1. *All loans*, both direct and dealer, will be point scored using the current tables as approved by the Installment Loan Department. Any loan not meeting the score requirements will be rejected unless written reasons for approval are shown on the application or investigation sheet.

2. Personal Loans—

a. Must score 60 points.

b. Get complete listing of all debts.

c. *NO* personal loans to be extended to individuals having household goods loans at loan companies.

d. No personal loans if the total of *all* monthly payments (excluding home mortgage) will exceed 25% of net income.

e. Get signatures of *both* husband and wife on note.

3. Automobile Loans—

a. Must score 50 points.

b. Complete description of car, including engine and major accessories, must be on application or investigation sheet.

c. Yegen Guide Figure or Red Book Loan Value must be shown.

d. Advances on New Cars—Yegen Guide with 10% LEEWAY.

e. Advances on used—Loan Value with 10% LEEWAY subject to inspection of car.

f. All used cars to be inspected on direct loans and on indirect where advisable.

g. MAXIMUM MATURITIES—

New Cars—36 Months

Used Cars—30 Months

Loans must be fully amortized in substantially equal payments. *NO BALLOONS.*

4. Collateral Loans on Household Goods—

a. Must score 60 points.

b. Get signatures of *both* husband and wife on note and security agreement.

5. Property Improvement Loans—

a. Must score 60 points.

b. Applications must be complete in every detail.

c. No advances for funds to be used for purposes other than improvement of the subject property.

d. No mortgages.

e. Husbands and wives must sign the note.

(Reproduced with permission of Mr. Robert J. Barth, President, The First National Bank, Dayton, Ohio.)

ORAN H. KITE

Credit Codes

PERHAPS THE FIRST THING we should do is to define our subject. Let us say it is practices and principles which will help insure better performance in handling the loan portfolio of each of our banks.

A credit code could easily cover a great number of matters, but we will discuss only a very few items in general terms. They may sound very elementary, and they are, but they don't have to be complex or sound highfalutin to be of value. There is nothing mysterious about sound loan policy.

The day-to-day responsibility for making sound loans rests with the active officers of the bank, but *they should have a sound loan policy established by the board to guide them.* And then their performance should be *regularly reviewed* by the board under clearly established routines and procedures. These should result in the board, or a selected committee of the board, being satisfied they are familiar with nearly all of the bank's loans, in terms of aggregate dollar amounts. As the bank's loans are made and as they are reviewed from time to time, *the board must in some manner participate* in both programs to fulfill its responsibilities adequately. As you review your responsibilities in this area, you must remember that all bank officers are not honest and all bank officers are not competent.

We will name and then elaborate a little on *just two elements of a credit code*:

1. *Make the loans right and with full knowledge of all related matters.* On the large percentage in amount of total loans, all the considerations which influence your decision, including the financial responsibility, information on character and ability, the use of loan proceeds, source and time of repayment, should be set out in full detail in the bank's records.

2. *Be sure a system is established* by which your officers and then you, as directors, *can and do follow the performance of the loans after they are made.*

Now, to get back to the first of the two points in our credit code, make the loans right in the first instance. I don't want to review all basic credit fundamentals, but an important part of your responsibility is to know that your loan officers are fully aware of these and follow them diligently.

There are two fundamentals which do not get as much attention as they deserve, but they are very important to most good loans and to their collection.

1. *Usually it is vital for a lender to have complete and detailed knowledge of the use to be made of the loan proceeds.*

2. *There should be a complete and detailed discussion of the source of funds with which a loan is to be repaid, and a clearly defined program as to when payments are to be made and in what amounts.*

These sound very simple, but they are of primary importance, and of course usually are closely related. *The value of these two considerations can hardly be overemphasized.*

If both of these matters are not part of the basic considerations regarding a loan on your books, then if it turns out to have been a good loan, it is more or less an accident.

The use of the loan proceeds may result in the loan being a short-term, seasonal working capital loan, or it may be for a fixed capital purpose. When the bank is going to get paid and where the money is coming from are completely different considerations in the two cases. If the banker and the director are subsequently to appraise the performance on a loan, then certainly these two facts must be clearly understood and spelled out in order that they may know what to expect. As an illustration, consider a loan to buy a truck. If the loan is to a truck dealer, then he expects to sell the truck soon and expects the sale to provide funds to pay the loan. If it is to the operator of a truckline, then he will ultimately pay the loan from cash flow as he uses the truck. The banker must expect payment only over an extended period.

The first principle of our credit code is merely a condensation of sound fundamentals—make the loans right with full knowledge of all facts, and spell out details in the records of each transaction.

The second element of a sound credit code is a system for following loan performance. If we presume for the moment that most loans are soundly made—and that may or may not be true in any bank—we still know that *conditions and people change and these changes influence a borrower's ability to repay a loan.* The banker and you as directors appraising loan performance should set up a program which informs you of changed conditions that will affect the performance of your loans. You must have knowledge of these changes so that the bank can take steps as promptly as possible to protect its loan before it is too late.

I don't think the relationship of lender and borrower is necessarily an "until death do us part" one; rather, it is one in which changed conditions warrant the adoption of different attitudes and new approaches to the problems which may arise as a result of change. Perhaps new approaches are required because of faulty judgment on our part in the first place.

There are numerous things which can be done which will help in this review of loan performance and materially improve a bank's overall credit results. A critical and objective program for review of loan performance and continuous basis should be established. In a large bank a separate and distinct division may perhaps be set up with only that responsibility. In a smaller bank such an approach is probably impractical, but some program for regular review should be established.

Full attention should be given to the bank's examiner's report and the loans mentioned in it. These are loans that have some undesirable aspects, or they would not be mentioned. Most of these examiners are good, capable men who are looking at the bank's loans objectively for the bank's benefit, and their opinions should be carefully considered. This report is of great value, if taken seriously, and all loans mentioned deserve new attention by the bank officers and directors. Once listed in the report, loans should be periodically reviewed as to their performance, and probably steps should be taken to improve the prospects of ultimate collection. At least set up a system by which you follow them regularly.

In every bank examination there are a number of loans which are discussed at considerable length by the bank examiner but not mentioned in the report. These should go on your special attention or "watch" list. There was a real reason for their having received so much attention.

If a banker waits for the bank examiner to point out his poor or substandard loans, he has waited too long. He has allowed a lot of time to be wasted, time during which perhaps many things could have been done to protect the bank and perhaps the customer as well.

As you know, the directors are required to make a periodic examination of the affairs of the bank. This should afford a fine opportunity for the officers and directors to establish another list of loans that deserve regular and special attention to insure payment.

The bank's officers and directors should have a much closer knowledge of the bank's loans than the examiner and *should recognize potential problems long before the examiner. If such is not the case, something is wrong.* So, in addition to the examiner's poor-loan list, set up your own problem-loan list, review it periodically, and see what has been done to insure ultimate collection. Add other loans as you recognize new problems.

You and your officers should regularly consider together:

1. Those *important loans* regarding which there has been a *material variance from the original payment schedule.* Why did the variance occur? If loan payments don't come in, we should know what occurred and see what steps should be taken. This is one of the reasons for paying so much attention to the payment program in the first place; don't ignore it now.

2. Another report which will be available and enlightening will be a monthly report on all loans which have been renewed x number of times without reasonable amount repaid. Set your own terms on this, but bear two things in mind: first, that without some check an alert and reasonably smart loan officer can keep a loan, or group of loans, secured only by blue sky, in the bank for years without detection. This report may well show loans on which only interest has been paid or perhaps added to the note and not paid at all. And second, keep in mind the simple fact that time alone may change ability to pay.

3. The officers and directors should regularly *see a list of past-due loans* (you set the minimum size) and, depending upon the particular circumstances, *know why they are there.* The reason may or may not be acceptable.

4. *A report on loans without up-to-date financial information should be reviewed periodically.* Such information is vital at the time a loan is made, and continues to be vital as long as the loan is on the books. The examiner does it—it's his job and yours as well. A loan on the books *without adequate financial information to support it is suspect.*

5. Secured loans offer a good way to make a bank feel fat and happy. But it is not necessarily so. We all know that values change for a variety of reasons. These should be reviewed periodically, whether the loan is due or not. Personally, I don't like secured loans without a defined and agreed-upon source of payment. It is almost an immutable law that a borrower will not want to pay if the collateral increases in value, because he would then have to pay a tax. On the other side, if the collateral values go down and the banker insists on a sale at a loss, he has made an enemy for life.

We have had a few simple examples that will keep officers and directors more aware of troubles and potential troubles. *Early knowledge of a critical problem will frequently be invaluable—but only if the banker is willing to do something about it,* to take whatever prudent steps may be needed to improve security, to get paid, or to improve prospects of payment. Loan review and all of the steps discussed are useless unless there is a willingness to take steps that are indicated.

Perhaps you do all of these things in your bank now—perhaps much more. If you don't, such a program, conscientiously followed, should result in your suffering fewer losses.

PART FOUR

Trust Operations

LEONARD W. HUCK

Trust Business

IT SEEMS that everyone else is looking at trust departments these days; so, as bank directors, if you have not paid close attention to yours recently, perhaps this is the time to become well acquainted with it. By others, I mean Representative Wright Patman, the Hunt Commission, the Securities Exchange Commission, the Federal Reserve Board, the Mutual Fund Industry, and many congressional task forces that suddenly have become fascinated with trust department activities.

The staff report of the House Domestic Finance Subcommittee includes such evaluations as:

1. "Bank dominance of the financial marketplace must be halted if the competitive character of our economy is to be sustained."

2. Trust departments are concentrating their investments in the stocks of relatively few large companies—the fifty largest for the most part. Thus, the market for the securities of hundreds of small corporations has been reduced, "diminishing the strength of the free enterprise system."

3. Enormous conflict-of-interest problems are created by the coexistence of commercial and trust departments within the same banking institution.

4. Trust department portfolio activities can be coordinated to benefit trust accounts at the expense of the banks' shareholders and depositors.

5. Trust department investments can be used to help "bail out" an ailing corporation which is heavily indebted to the commercial department of the bank.

6. Loans can be withheld from competitors of corporations which are heavily represented in the investment portfolios of trust accounts, thereby diminishing ability to compete.

This report was bound to have an impact on the hearings before the full House Banking Committee, chaired by Representative Wright Patman, and when it concluded with "there is no effective way of preventing the exchange of such information between the commercial bank and the trust bank when the will and the temptation are both present," it left banking in a rather suspect position.

In the interest of semantics, it might be said that no bank has a trust department; rather, it has a fiduciary department. Our banks serve in fiduciary capacities for our customers. Fiduciary means having trust or confidence, and this "service for the benefit of another person" is very evident in every capacity in which banks serve—whether as trustee, executor, administrator, guardian, agent, or registrar of stocks and bonds.

If this is the case, how did we become known as trust departments? Trust is a creature of English common law. It has no civil law counterpart. In the conduct of their businesses, trust institutions are governed by the cardinal principle that is common to all fiduciary relationships—namely, fidelity. Policies predicated upon this principle have as their objectives safety, good management, and the ultimate in personal service. Many years ago it was established that when a bank, or a person for that matter, acts in a fiduciary capacity, the very existence of that relationship of trust and confidence absolutely prohibits any transaction by the fiduciary which involves self-dealing or conflict of interest. These are the suspects of certain of the extensive studies to which I have referred.

Unless one actually has lived in the environment of a trust department, it is probably difficult to appreciate the respect with which trust officers hold the basic trust principles. The courts have deliberately made loyalty to the interests of a beneficiary, at the expense of the fiduciary's personal interest, the overriding concern. Further, the court has said that it is the duty of the fiduciary to use all the ability which he personally has—and if the fiduciary does a poor job—i.e., does not use all his ability—he can be surcharged for the resulting loss.

How did this highly respected corporate fiduciary concept develop? It seems to have paralleled the growth of the corporate organization, free enterprise, and the acquisition of individual capital in America. As individual fortunes were amassed as a result of the industrial revolution, the strong human desire to preserve one's family wealth brought about a need for the immortality and stability of a professional corporate fiduciary. The other ingredient which could best be supplied by a corporate fiduciary was expertise. Only professionals could provide the highly technical skills required in fiduciary relationships. There was no doubt that the need existed for some entity to deal with the increasing complexity of assets, and also to cope with the mobility of beneficiaries which began to typify affluent America in the 1800s.

First, insurance companies created anuities in trust; and soon they were administering estates and inter vivos trusts. With the increased growth of industry and the corporate structure, there developed a need for corporate trust services, such as bond indenture trustees, transfer agents, and registrars. As the trust business became profitable, some of these insurance companies phased out of their conventional insurance activities and became trust companies. Their creativity resulted in variations of their annuities in trusts, referred to as annuity contracts and deposits in trust. Eventually, the trust companies found themselves in deposit banking.

With the enactment of the free banking laws, deposit banks began to look at trust business; and by the end of the nineteenth century trust companies were well established in banking, and state banks were well established in the trust business. National banks did not gain trust powers until the passage of the Federal Reserve Act in 1913. This act became the reference point for all banks in the operation of trust departments, since the regulatory powers which were applied by the Federal Reserve affected state member banks as well as national banks.

Just four years after the Federal Reserve Act became effective in 1913, there was an amendment to the act which stipulated that separate books and records must be kept for the trust department. This has resulted in the complete physical separation of some commercial and trust banks. The recognition of this moral partition between the commercial and trust banks makes it all the harder to acknowledge the value in some of the research projects that are under way through government commissions.

Banks must pledge securities as collateral for trust funds on deposit in the commercial side of their organization. The loan of trust funds to directors, officers, and employees of the trustee bank has been a criminal offense since the passage of the 1913 Federal Reserve Act. Allocating brokerage commissions resulting from transactions in trust accounts on the basis of the deposit balances maintained by broker customers is a "no-no." These and other strong regulations act as a wedge in separating the commercial bank from the trust bank.

Comprehensive and scholarly addresses have been made on the advantages and disadvantages of structurally segregating the trust bank and the commercial bank. I hope this will not become another case of throwing out the baby with the bathwater. There are so many advantages to customers that result from trust services and commercial banking services being offered by the same institution that banks ought not to let a very few abuses spoil a good thing for their customers. Applications by national banks for permits to exercise fiduciary powers are looked at from many angles, not the least of which is the consideration of the adequacy of the bank's capital to stand behind the discretionary acts of the trust departments. Even in a business where integrity is the compelling discipline, it is reassuring to the customers to know that the bank's total capital and surplus are at risk if improper exercise of fiduciary powers should be proved. In the event of mandatory separation, one of the first problems would be arriving at a capital figure small enough to enable the trust business to provide an attractive return on invested capital, yet large enough to inspire public confidence. Today, bank capital is used for dual purposes, supporting both bank and trust activities. Separation would drain the bank capital, thus potentially affecting lending limits, stock prices, debt rating, divided policies, and acquisition plans. The rule of thumb most often referred to in estimating the capital requirement of an individual trust operation is two times the five-year average of gross trust revenue.

The responsibilities and liabilities of bank directors which apply specifically to trust duties are set forth in Regulation 9 of the Comptrollers Manual for National Banks:

1. The Board of Directors is responsible for the proper exercise of fiduciary powers by the bank. This includes the determination of policies, the investment and disposition of property held in a fiduciary capacity, and the direction and review of the action of all officers, employees and committees utilized by the bank in exercise of its fiduciary powers.

Fortunately, the Regulation goes on to say:

In discharging this responsibility, the Board of Directors may assign, by action duly entered in the minutes, the administration of such of the bank's fiduciary powers as it may consider proper to assign to such directors, officers, employees or committees as it may designate.

2. No fiduciary account shall be accepted without the prior approval of the

board or the officers or committees to whom the board may have designated the performance of that responsibility.

3. The board also shall insure that at least once during every calendar year, and within 15 months of the last review, all assets held in each fiduciary account where the bank has investment responsibilities are reviewed to determine the advisability of retaining or disposing of such assets.

4. All officers and employees taking part in the operation of the trust department shall be adequately bonded.

5. Every national bank exercising fiduciary powers must have competent legal counsel.

6. Every national bank shall maintain a record of all pending litigation to which it is a party in connection with its exercise of fiduciary powers.

7. A committee of directors, exclusive of any active officers of the bank, shall at least once during each calendar year, and within 15 months of the last such audit, make or cause to be made, suitable audits of the trust department.

Despite these specific and rather burdensome responsibilities, Regulation 9 has given more freedom to boards of directors in carrying out their authority than did its forerunner, Federal Regulation F. The common trust funds regulations were liberalized, the Trust Investment Committee was reduced from a requirement of the board to a delegated responsibility, and the acceptance and closing of trusts became in reality a committee function rather than a direct board responsibility. The Comptroller recognized the merits of issuing a manual of instructions for Representatives in Trusts, which really is an authoritative interpretation of Regulation 9, as well as the instruction book for the Federal Trust Examiners. It sets forth many regulatory requirements and guidelines, and also reproduces all of the questions in the National Bank Trust Department Report of Examination. In other words, this manual shows what the examiner is looking for, and there is no reason why every trust department should not have the manual readily available to assure proper trust administration.

At one of the first Assemblies for Bank Directors, Dean Miller, Deputy Comptroller for Trusts, said:

> Most breakdowns in trust departments result from the failure of the directors to acquaint themselves with the basic fiduciary principles. Decisions in a trust department must be completely divorced from the considerations of the commercial side of the bank, with the sole reference point being the purpose of the individual account and the wellbeing of its beneficiaries.

What do these responsibilities which have been placed upon directors really mean? First, the acceptance of trusts suggests that directors should have someone scrutinize very closely the new business that is offered to a trust department before it is actually accepted. Directors can weed out some unprofitable business and perhaps avoid potential lawsuits at this point in the procedure. Prior approval on all accounts is an absolute must.

Second, be certain that your investment function is specifically assigned to competent trust investment officers and that invesment reviews of the accounts are held in a timely fashion. Be certain that an annual audit is held by a committee of the directors or by competent auditors whom you may direct to make such an audit. Be sure that initial reviews are held just as soon as possible after acceptance of the account to assure that all account assets have been obtained and that they have been set up properly on your books. This would include the registration of the assets in the bank's name as fiduciary. Be sure that all cash is invested promptly and that substandard assets are converted to quality assets. Be sure that real estate is appraised regularly and that adequate insurance is maintained. Watch for improper investment in stock of the fiduciary bank. Specific authority in the governing instrument, or a court order, is required for this kind of an investment.

Be concerned about the voting of stock of the fiduciary bank. In national banks a provision of the national banking act prevents voting of stock held in trust in the election of directors, except in certain situations. In other words, the bank in its fiduciary capacity must vote the stock of the fiduciary bank solely with reference to the purposes of the account and the interests of the beneficiary. Be alert for transactions which could be considered self-dealing, such as purchases or sales to the trust department which appear to serve the interests of the bank and which could result in the trust department's coming out second best. Pension and profit-sharing trusts should be mentioned, as these are frequently the target of examiners. Remember that employers cannot use pension or profit-sharing trusts as another source of capital. Sometimes an effort to accomplish this manifests itself in broad authorities and exculpatory clauses in the governing instrument, but from all that I can learn this is an invitation for trouble. Pension and profit-sharing trusts must be administered for the exclusive benefit of the employees.

What about the profitability of trust departments? The Federal Reserve Bank of New York's annual survey of trust department earnings and expenses for 1972 showed that ten large New York City Bank Trust Departments earned aggregate net operating profits of $5.2 million compared to a net operating deficit of $18.3 million in 1971. The operating profit was the first since 1968, when it totaled $6.8 million.

After the addition of allowed credits for deposits, trust departments' net earnings for these ten New York City banks totaled $111 million. This is good news, one might say; trust departments have finally shrugged off the image of being a burden on the bank's profit objectives. Unfortunately, this war has not been completely won; but we do have a battle or two to our credit.

In the same survey, 108 trust departments, excluding the 10 large New York City banks, showed their aggregate expenses exceeded their total fees and commissions by 1.5%. Here again, credit for deposits brought final trust department net earnings to 26.8%. Exactly half of the 108 reporting departments showed net operating losses before allowed credits for deposits. Even after the credits, 23 departments continued to show a loss.

If profitability is a problem even in the large metropolitan banks, why are we in the trust business? Among the Federal Reserve Act the criteria listed for banks qualified to exercise fiduciary powers was the need of the community for a corporate fiduciary. At this point in time, almost ⅓ of the commercial banks of the nation, or about 4,200 banks, are operating trust departments. Of these, 2,500, or about 60%, have trust assets with book values of $10,000,000 or less, and are troubled by chronic department unprofitability. Quite naturally, this results in the management and boards of directors of these banks relegating the trust functions to a status where they are grudgingly tolerated but not promoted. I invite you as a bank director to learn enough about your trust departments so that you can understand the problems blocking their way to profitability and recognize their virtues so that you will help promote them into profitability. First of all, you should examine your own situation. Have you named your bank as executor of your estate? Do you have, or have you made plans to have, a living trust or an agency account managed in your bank's trust department? If you are in business, is your bank serving as trustee for your employee profit sharing plan or pension plan? If your business has the need for corporate trust services, such as stock transfer agency, registrar, dividend paying agency, bond trustee, and related services, is your bank providing these services? If by chance you have not been able to answer "yes" to each of these, I would like to examine with you the possible reasons.

Do you by any chance lack confidence in the people who are performing the trust functions in your bank? Is this because you have not made it a point to get acquainted with them and thereby to learn of their areas of specialization? Or is it a result of your knowledge of the salary structure in your trust department, which causes you to conclude that attorneys, investment officers, property managers, and tax specialists working at these salaries could not possibly represent the very best in their respective fields? Trust is a highly specialized service and requires real experts if we are to deserve the confidence of people in our communities who could benefit from trust services.

If you represent one of the ten thousand commercial banks that do not have a trust department, please give careful consideration to the man you select to start it. He must be a salesman to bring in trust business, an investment man to know how to manage the assets held in trust, an operations man to keep accurate records and see that errorless reports are rendered, a tax man for obvious reasons; he must either be a lawyer or be a person very familiar with law applying to trusts and estates; and, of course, he should have a working knowledge of accounting. Please don't try to get him for a $12,000 per year salary.

It will continue to be difficult for your trust departments to acquire the volume of new accounts that they need to become profitable if they cannot command the attention and the commitment of their board members.

If you answer "no" to some of the questions posed earlier, perhaps another of the reasons had to do with the quality of reports or the sophistication of some of the services offered in your trust department. Encourage your management to review with your trust department manager the methods, procedures, and equipment your trust officers use. Although expense controls are as critical in bringing about profitability in the trust department as in any other department of the bank, too frequently bank managers are not aware of the modern operational techniques which could result in increased business, increased efficiency, and increased profits. Although trust is an extremely personal service, a large volume of items must be handled on a low unit cost basis. An optimum staff productivity is mandatory if profitable operations are to be achieved.

There is the possibility that your "no" was predicated on the fee structure that may have been quoted to you. As a converted commercial banker with a pretty good idea of the commercial banking services, I can say unequivocally that the trust services in most banks are the best bargains in your total inventory. In fact, it is very possible that your fee schedules are inadequate! In some cases this is due to statutory legislation; but in many others it is due to the competition having set these prices, rather than to the costs of the services being known and an appropriate markup added into the price tab for the customers. Think of the plight of your trust department in trying to reach profitability when management and directors too often ask for concessions on fees for the commercial bank customers who have valued commercial bank relationships. How many services does your trust department provide the commercial bank without compensation? How does this affect the profitability potential in your trust department? Very often trust departments are asked to help with tax returns, escrows, securities safekeeping, investment transactions, stock transfer service, preparation of the bank's own dividend checks, and many other services without compensation.

I encourage you to have your trust department personnel implement some kind of cost system so that you may learn the actual costs of administering each type of trust account. When you know what it costs to administer each individual account, reexamine your bank's fee schedule to see if it is consistent with management's objective for trust department profitability. Some have said that a trust department cannot possibly reach profitability until the assets under management aggregate from $5,000,000 up to $20,000,000, depending on the formula used. Others say profitability will not come until after annual income has hit $75,000. Others use the size of the community as the measuring device and suggest that a trust department cannot be profitable unless the community it services numbers at least 25,000 people. These are considerations if your bank does not have a trust department; but it is a good bit harder to get out of the trust business than to get into it, so if you already are exercising trust powers, learn the costs incident thereto.

If profitability is not the motivation for a trust department, what do we have to recommend the service we perform? Consider the following as just a few advantages:

1. A trust department makes a bank a completely integrated finan-

cial institution and broadens the potential sources of business for the bank as a whole.

2. Your trust department, if performing its job competently, retains business in all departments of the bank by creating and strengthening customer relationships.

3. It is an important source of deposits in your bank, as normal trust administration creates a large number of small trust balances, and their concentration in one fund very likely identifies the trust department as being the largest depositor in your bank.

4. Your trust department brings prestige and good will to your bank, and should generate confidence and respect in the eyes of your bank's customers as well as in the eyes of the general public.

5. It may very likely have the opportunity to perpetuate existing businesses that are bank customers by providing continuity of management during changes of ownership or in passing the business from generation to generation.

6. Finally, it does have the potential of being the source of worthwhile earnings in your bank.

Since I have alluded to the sizable number of unprofitable trust departments, this in itself may be ample evidence that many directors evaluate the other reasons as adequate justification for a chronically unprofitable trust operation. This unprofitability can become self-perpetuating, however, as management may become increasingly parsimonious in budgeting funds for competent trust personnel, modern equipment, and adequate supplies. Under these circumstances, it is inevitable that the quality of trust administration, as well as the business development thrust, would become diluted, and there would be no way for the department to improve its performance. With the gradual loss of effectiveness, it becomes less attractive to trust prospects; and when the quality of trust service becomes marginal, this in itself could impair the reputation of your entire bank. No bank can afford a cheap trust department; unless a bank can afford to pay salaries commensurate with the quality of work and the degree of responsibility expected of trust officers, it simply should not engage in trust business.

The following statement of principles of trust institutions was adopted in 1933:

A trust institution is entitled to reasonable compensation for its services. Compensation should be determined on the basis of the cost of the service rendered and the responsibility assumed. Minimum fees for trust services should be applied uniformly and impartially to all of its customers alike. A trust institution is under no obligation, either moral or legal, to accept all business that is offered.

In summary, let me repeat:

1. Everyone is looking at trust department activities. Mr. Patman's staff suggests a Federal Trust Management Commission to regulate and supervise the management of all foundations, charitable trusts, and pension funds. It has been suggested that investment advisory corporations be licensed to manage all pension, foundation, and charitable trust investments. With these functions removed from bank trust departments as we know them, the next recommendation is to separate completely from the commercial bank all trust departments holding $200 million or more in assets.

Federal Reserve Governor Jeff Bucher, a former trust officer himself, recommends that trust operations be spun off to separate bank subsidiary units in order to forestall more drastic remedies. Holding companies may be the answer to growing public doubt about bank-operated trust departments.

Chairman Ray Garrett of the Securities and Exchange Commission has gone before Congress to read a carefully worded statement depicting his increasing apprehension about the growing power of banks in the securities market.

The Securities Industry Association and the Investment Company Institute are pleading with Comptroller of the Currency James E. Smith to rescind his predecessor's ruling that automatic stock purchase plans are appropriate and legal activities for National Bank Trust Departments.

Deputy Comptroller of the Currency for Trusts Dean E. Miller is reemphasizing the prohibition in Regulation 9 against advertisement of common trust funds, including reports of trust department holdings. At the same time, our new President of the Trust Division of the American Bankers Association, Chalkley Hambleton, reminds us that confidence is required to get individuals into the stock market. If disclosure will help build consumer confidence in our securities markets, he believes it is worth the administrative and economic costs to institutional investors, so long as disclosure is limited to significant data.

The Uniform Probate Code now in effect in Idaho and Alaska has been enacted in Arizona, Colorado, and North Dakota. Bills incorporating the code have been introduced in at least fifteen other states.

Pension legislation affecting vesting, funding, portability, plan termination insurance, and fiduciary standards seem headed for enactment this year.

In other words, with this much fascination with your trust department activities, you had better know a lot about what goes on there.

2. Fiduciary responsibilities are awesome, and your trust personnel are as dedicated to sound trust principles as they are formally trained to perform their specialities. Understand and respect them for that commitment.

3. The corporate fiduciary developed out of a need for immortality, stability, and expertise through a relationship of trust and confidence which absolutely prohibits any transaction involving self-dealing or conflict of interest.

4. Your bank directors are specifically charged with responsibility to see that your bank properly exercises its fiduciary powers.

5. Trust departments do have other virtues to recommend them besides profitability, but properly organized and operated they can be a significant source of bank earnings.

6. It will be very difficult for your trust department to acquire the volume and quality of new accounts needed to make the department profitable if they cannot command the attention and the commitment from their own bank directors.

REESE H. HARRIS, JR.

Importance of a Strong Trust Department

PLUTARCH, in his *Life of Caesar*, says that when Caesar was asked why he parted with his wife, he replied, "I wished my wife to be not so much as suspected." Anyone who has been following events in the banking business during the last six or seven years would agree that on that principle, banks and their trust departments would long ago have been divorced. Which of the parties would have played the role of Caesar in that litigation is not clear, but that only shows that no metaphor can be carried to extremes. Caesar's harsh principle is an impossible ideal, of course. No one is above suspicion, nor should he be. There are, however, degrees of skepticism, and I think Caesar meant to say that his wife should be so exemplary in her conduct that rational observers would have no reason to suspect it.

Applying that standard to banks and their trust departments, can we say that suspicion of us is completely irrational? You may be surprised when I say I think it is not at all irrational. I propose here to indicate what it is we are suspected of, and by whom, with what possible consequences; and then to suggest some things banks might do to bring their trust operations more nearly to the Caesarean ideal.

The general term usually applied to criticisms of banks and their trust departments is "conflicts of interest," which fairly well describes the suspected wrongdoing which deserves serious consideration. It does not, however, include everyone's catalog of our supposed misdeeds. There is another category which I have dubbed "influence-wielding and nonwielding." This category has two distinct parts and two high priests. One part is affirmative: influence-wielding, with overtones of conflicts of interest, and this school is the province of Chairman Patman. The other part is negative: the failure to wield influence in certain socially desirable directions, and Ralph Nader is the principal exponent of these views. Influence wielding and nonwielding by banks and their trust departments cannot be neglected, if only because of the importance of the exponents of this category, but it is not nearly so serious a subject as that of conflicts of interest has always been and will always be.

Mr. Patman is not alone either in historical perspective or with his contemporaries. He is a populist, and he has lots of company in his views. His great fear is of concentration of economic power. While most Americans share this fear, few think today that worrisome concentrations of economic power wielded surreptitiously for selfish, evil reasons exist, as he thinks they do. He thinks that banks, particularly the large ones, basically run the country, and that is why in 1967 his Subcommittee on Domestic Finance investigated the question of the control of commerical banks by "analyzing in detail the ownership pattern of 48 banks in 10 major population centers. . . ." In that connection, he ran into trust department holdings of their own and others' bank stock, particularly in pension and profit sharing funds. This led to the study issued in 1968 entitled "Commercial Banks and Their Trust Activities: Emerging Influence on the American Economy." Both of these reports were useful contributions, though not for the reason of their authors' conclusions. Their usefulness lies both in the factual data made available for the first time about bank ownership and the trust business, and in the failure to prove the propositions the subcommittee tried so hard to prove.

But the suspicions remain with people like Chairman Patman. They simply cannot believe, for example, that a bank which has as much airline stock as Morgan Guaranty had, or has, in its trust department accounts will not be wheeling and dealing with the stock to produce competitive advantages between the different lines, or to make or break engine and airplane manufacturers, or at least to develop deposit and loan business for its banking operation. This situation is not the exclusive province of big banks, either. The same concentrations of local stocks in a local trust department produce the same suspicions. For many people these suspicions are facts which must be true, and all that is lacking is the proof. The possession of power and its abuse are not, indeed, all that far apart, and it is foolish to dismiss the Wright Patman attitude toward the banks and trust business airily by quoting the motto of the British Crown, *Honi soit qui mal y pense,* or "Evil be to him who thinks evil."

The Ralph Naders criticize banks for *not* exercising their alleged economic power, particularly in trust stockholdings, to produce better cars, a pollution-free environment, an end to the war in Vietnam, and social revolution in far-off lands. Unlike Patman, the Naders are not suspicious of evildoing, unless you can call it evil not to vote stock held in trust or deliberately to withhold credit in order to produce socially desirable results. The banks should, in my opinion, make it clear that they think they have neither the right nor the competence to vote against management on these issues. I think that if we ever get to voting other people's stock for what we regard as socially desirable objectives, or for any reason other than what is best for our customers, we will quickly lose to others, probably the government, the right to vote at all, and perhaps lose the customers as well. We will be jumping from the Nader pan into the Patman fire. The consumerism movement and the social activists will be with us for a long time and will produce political and emotional problems requiring much self-restraint. But to me it is so clear that we should not give in to the Nader type of criticism that it is hard for me to take it seriously. (A related problem, which must be taken seriously, and which is difficult if not impossible to solve, is the customer who *wants* the trust department, in its investment of his money, to pursue not just investment results but also some other social policy objectives. This problem is not new; for example, there is the church-related fund that shuns tobacco and alcohol stocks, or the Christian Scientist who doesn't want drug stocks. In today's world of corporate conglomeration, it becomes very difficult to do good investing and comply with such rules, yet the business importance of the customer may require the effort.)

The strength of these criticisms of the trust business, unlike the conflict of interest criticism, is directly proportional to the amount of property managed by the banks. It is no coincidence that these issues have come to the fore in two decades when trust assets increased from $25 billion to $280 billion. And as these assets are increasing at a compound annual rate of 10 percent, concentrated among fifty to one hundred trust institutions, the horsepower behind these contentions is bound to increase. The importance of these criticisms as concerns for the banking and trust business is not so much their inherent merit, because there isn't much of that, but the political fact of their continued existence.

On the other hand, the conflict of interest criticism of the banks and their trust departments has always had merit and does not depend for its vigor on the size of the assets under management. As the poet said: "The quality of mercy is not strained. . . ." and neither is the quality of fiduciary conduct. One slight deviation from the straight and narrow path of proper fiduciary conduct is one too many. For some people the answer to conflict of interest problems is not to have any conflicts of interest. Unfortunately, life is not that simple. There is no way for a professional fiduciary to avoid the existence of conflict of interest situations both between different fiduciary relationships and between fiduciary relations and the trustee's personal interests. They are bound to arise; the important question is whether they can be managed properly, which is, of course, in all cases in the best interests of the trust beneficiaries.

Perhaps examples of typical conflict of interest problems might help us to understand the situation. They come in infinite and sometimes baffling forms, but the essence of all of them is that the bank is tempted to utilize in some way its position as a fiduciary for its individual profit. Getting and keeping profitable banking business is a daily concern of a commercial bank officer; there are many opportunities to do bank customers favors with trust assets. A good customer wants to get a preferred position in buying a piece of real estate which a trust account has for sale; a business corporation wants a combination of short- and long-term credit, and somebody else's pension fund finds the long-term credit as an investment; a real estate firm gets appraisal work and listings from the trust department in exchange for its rent collection deposit; political favors can be exchanged for trust department patronage. What about building deposit business with trust brokerage commissions? This allegedly violates the antitrust laws, but it is not also a breach of trust? The list is endless, but it is no more endless than the list of similar kinds of opportunities to be unethical in many other businesses. And even if we didn't have to be alert to our own possible wrongdoing, a trustee must be alert to that of his cofiduciaries, because knowledge of a breach of trust by a cofiduciary or by a fiduciary customer and acquiescence in it, even without any benefit, subjects you to the same penalties as if you were guilty and had benefited. Even if a bank had no conflicts of interest involving its trust department, it would still have a need for a sophisticated awareness of the problems and of the right responses.

At the present time I think the trust business has come out of a period of severe investigation and criticism practically unscathed. The most recent such experience, which must have cost the fifty largest trust banks at least ten million dollars, was the SEC's Institutional Investor Study. The main thrust of this effort was the impact of institutional investors—mutual funds, insurance companies, investment advisors, foundations and trust funds—on the stock market. However, it spent much time in examining, in the trust field, issues of conflicts of interest, reciprocity in broker relationships, investment performance, fee schedules, and earnings. As I have said, the study found no serious fault with us. But it was largely based on huge amounts of data analyzed by computer. Whether we would come off as well in another kind of investigation—say of the Penn Central type—is not to be taken for granted from our success in this one. While this is a very creditable situation, I do not think it is any ground for complacency. Frankly, I think we have been pretty lucky. *If we want to continue our traditional trust business without any more governmental interference than we have now, and enjoy the continued confidence of our customers* (and this is my point), we must organize our trust departments within the bank so that top management can be assured that it will see, and have the opportunity to deal properly with, all the issues of conflicts of interest and of influence-wielding and nonwielding. I don't think trust department organization has up to now been considered in that light. Trust departments have been structured like other departments in the bank, or just "grew" like Topsy, or are the product of the interaction of differing personalities. Some of these factors will, of course, continue to influence the structuring of trust organizations; but I submit that the importance of creating an organization which assures proper trust management by a bank must today be uppermost in the minds of those who are responsible. I don't want to give the impression that I advocate this merely to avoid more government regulation, or to avoid political criticism. Basically, I advocate this because I think our trust customers are more sensitive to conflict of interest issues than the politicians, and their confidence is of much greater importance to us. In fact, it is the *sine qua non* of our business because the continuation of as much as 75 percent of our business is in the discretion of the customer.

How can we arrange the management of our trust responsibilities so that conflict of interest problems are recognized and correctly solved and so that we can assure our customers that this is so? Perhaps what we need is the managerial equivalent of our ancestors' bundling board, used to separate bank from trust. What is a bundling board? According to Henry Reed Stiles, in his book *Bundling and More about Bundling*, bundling was the custom in the early days in New England of a man and a woman lying in the same bed with their clothes on. Sometimes the lady wore a special kind of sleeping bag with a drawstring. Nothing was supposed to happen between the two except talk, but the problem was to assure this. Dr. Stiles's editor, Mr. A. Munro Awrand, Jr., says:

> Another entirely different sort of arrangement existed at one time in parts of Pennsylvania tending to show what may have been said to be either a suspicious attitude toward bundling, or else was intended to give a guaranteed amount of bed space to each occupant of whatever sex. We refer to the centerboard. . . . No regular height of the board is given, but is estimated to vary from 12 to 18 inches and to run the full length from head to foot between sleepers. With this extra protection, the girls had also a good physical constitution and a stout set of lungs, and usually a father and several brothers, to come to her aid, if necessary in times of difficulty.

The most obvious and simplistic solution to the bundling problem and the trust problem is total divestment for trust departments and separate bedrooms for bundlers (should we call it "unbundling"?) and a number of observers have advocated total divestment for the trust business. Like curing a sore throat with the guillotine, this is a pretty radical and, in my view, entirely unnecessary solution. The arguments against it are powerful and too numerous for me to go into here. I might add that some would advocate the separation of trust business from banking for another reason—that our utilization of uninvested cash from trust accounts gives us in the banking business an unfair competitive advantage over nonbank entities seeking to do a trust business. If we don't strengthen our managerial arrangements or if we are unlucky in the future, I'm sure that government-mandated divestiture of trust business from banking could be the result.

What less than divestiture will assure both good fiduciary management in fact and the confidence of our customers? I think the proper structuring of the fiduciary activities of the bank is one half of the solution, and the proper indoctrination of all personnel is the other half.

It is my opinion, first, that except for the chief executive officer, no employee of a bank should have a mixture of bank and trust responsibilities, and second, that the proper structure of a trust function in a bank, one which is entitled to be called a trust department, is the assembly of all personnel who perform nothing but fiduciary functions under one individual who of course has no other banking responsibilities and who reports directly to the chief executive officer. His title must reflect this stature. Preferably he should be *ex officio* a member of the bank's board (and if HR 5700 were enacted, there would be plenty of room on a typical bank board for the head of the trust department). With that assist to my old friends in the trust business must go this kicker: now that it doesn't matter personally to me, and from personal experience, I think no trust department official should be a member of the board of directors of a portfolio company, unless the bank is prepared to admit that the size of the trust department's holdings constitutes possible control or unless the company is privately owned. The trust department should be so well integrated that if divestment of trust functions were ordered, the lines of cleavage would be clear and the entity divested largely viable on its own (except for capital).

A strong case could be made for the proposition that the trust department should be a separate corporate entity, either a subsidiary of the bank or a subsidiary of the bank's holding company. Then a separate trust board could be assembled and given responsibility for trust matters including conflicts of interest with the bank. The analogy of the investment company's unaffiliated directors will come to mind here. Such a separate entity could have its own salary policies, including incentive compensation. I note that Citizens & Southern of Atlanta has set up an investment counseling service to manage C & S trust assets; its vice-president Charles W. Brady said: "It seems to me that this is at least half of what Patman wants." I would say one-tenth is a nearer guess. A big difficulty with separate incorporation, however, is the necessity of dividing the bank's capital between trust and banking. The customers of both sides will not be made any happier thereby. Another disadvantage would be the loss of mutual support inevitably resulting from too much separateness in areas where collaboration between banking and trust is entirely proper and even vital.

But if separate incorporation is not the answer, I think many of its advantages can be achieved by consciously creating a really integrated trust department. Too many banks have in effect several trust divisions, typically split up among corporate trust, personal trust, employee benefit plans, custodial, investment, and operations—some reporting to separate officers who may or may not also have nontrust duties. All of these divisions should report to one man *who has no other duties but fiduciary duties.* He then personally has no conflicts of interest between his banking and fiduciary responsibilities.

The other principle which will go far to assure the proper management of conflicts of interest between bank and trust is that all hands, particularly trust, shall be well indoctrinated in the problem. The chief executive officer must be very well aware that the crunch between duty and self-interest will be his eventually and that he needs a powerful keeper of his conscience, like the king's chancellor. As I have said, the head of the trust department must have a title which reflects this responsibility. The trust department should, through its head, be encouraged to be stiff-necked and "uncooperative," whenever, but only whenever, potential conflict problems come up. All personnel, bank and trust, must be aware that communication between the two must be guarded, particularly in the sensitive areas of credit information and investment decisions. At one point we all thought that the answer to conflict of interest problems was to be found in the erection of a communications barrier between the two sides, the so-called "Chinese Wall." But as Henry Harfield pointed out in an article in the *Banking Law Journal* in 1969, the wall is neither possible, desirable, nor credible. Messrs. Herman and Safanda, working under the aegis of the Center for the Study of Financial Institutions, came to much the same conclusion in their paper entitled "Commercial Bank Trust Department and the 'Wall.'" There are practical problems in the daily physical proximity and friendships of trust and banking personnel that would make an absolute lack of communication impossible. Moreover, there are many instances in which communication is proper, and in some it is vitally necessary. And even if we tried, our critics, juries, and politicians wouldn't believe it. No, we need much more sophisticated techniques than just severely buttoned-up lips.

I know just how difficult it is to put people lower down in the hierarchy of an organization, and what I suggest here amounts to just that in many banks. Where more than one person has been reporting to the president or a vice-chairman or even the chairman about trust matters, they would now be reporting to a man who has no other duties in the bank, who will then be reporting to the chairman or chief executive officer. While one of these people will probably be selected to be that new officer, the move will be regarded as a demotion not only for those who report lower down in the hierarchy, but for their whole divisions. If trust operations are handled in the bank's operations group, special reasons will be found for not having to report to the head of the trust department. But the only way a chief executive officer can really be sure that conflicts of interest will be properly managed is to have one man in charge of them who has no personal bank vs. trust conflict problem. And if economic influence-wielding is to be credibly nonexistent, it must be because there is a guardian of the proper use of trust investments who would have to cooperate if an improper use of trust investments, such as influence-wielding, were proposed.

The proper management of a bank's fiduciary obligations, particularly in the field of conflicts of interest, is the best reason for a truly integrated trust department. I think, however, that such a form of organization is the only way to get good service for customers, good investing, and general overall efficiency and high morale.

I believe, therefore, that our trust departments face three kinds of critics today: those who do not believe that we manage our conflicts of interest problems properly in all instances, those who believe that our trust assets enable us to wield economic power for selfish ends, and those who believe we should wield economic power for socially desirable ends. These critics must be taken seriously. To date these criticisms have not been substantiated, but we may not always be so lucky. We must make sure that our trust departments are so well integrated and indoctrinated that the proper management of conflicts of interest and economic power will be no accident, and when we claim that this is the case, we will be believed by all fair-minded people.

WILL MANN RICHARDSON

Why Should Small Trust Departments Lose Money?

THERE ARE FAR MORE small trust departments than large, and yet numerous surveys indicate that most of the small operations are unprofitable. Despite those unhappy statistics, experience and observation have convinced us that sound management and hard work can convert an overwhelming majority of trust departments into money-makers by a realistic analysis of their problems and opportunities. There may be rare exceptions, but as a general rule we believe that a trust department can and should be required to earn a profit in order to justify its continuance after the first few inevitably lean years.

Several reasons are frequently cited for keeping an unprofitable small trust department. Of such advantages usually claimed, only one is measureable in dollars: the bank deposits created by balances belonging to trust funds. The rest of the alleged benefits are in the field of intangibles. All of them can be lumped together as various aspects of the fostering of public relations and the strengthening of customer relationships.

Perhaps it would be unduly skeptical to dismiss the lot as mere rationalization of an undesirable situation. Certainly, however, it is a fair guess that very few if any of today's unprofitable trust departments were established in their yesterdays for any purpose other than to make money for the bank by earning more in fees than the amount that would be spent for expense. That the departments fail to achieve this goal would seem to warrant asking, in each instance, whether the bank would voluntarily budget the same amount of annual expense to purchase benefits identical to those now claimed.

Another question worth asking in this connection is, can an undersized and almost surely undernourished trust department really build public and customer goodwill? The fact is that many, perhaps most, small trust departments are typical examples of economic malnutrition. Because the trust operation loses money, the bank's board of directors cuts down on the trust budget, personnel, and supplies. In consequence, the weakened department becomes even less well equipped than before to give good service to its customers or acquire new business to support future growth. The ailments in turn increase the likelihood—indeed the certainty—of continuing losses.

When I have the opportunity to speak to a group of trust men or bank directors, my theme is likely to deal with the conviction that only the board of directors can break the downward spiral of such a deteriorating situation. What the directors know, think, and do in relation to the trust department holds the key to that unit's success or failure. It is up to the bank's management, particularly the trust department's management, to make sure that the directors develop attitudes and actions which will enable the trust operation to cross the break-even line.

Consider the problem that faced one trust officer who came into an unprofitable department determined to get it out of the red ink without delay. It was a relatively new venture, and its principal difficulties were clearly due to insufficient volume. He proceeded to strengthen the department and improve its service. When the board's executive committee met each week he sat down with its five members to review the departmental progress and, he hoped, so convince them of its competence that they would spread the word among their predominantly prosperous friends in the community. Three of the five, all of them elderly, died during his first two years on the job. It turned out that not one of the three had appointed the bank in any trust capacity.

The trust officer ruefully reported:

> When the word got around, I estimated this set back our program of new business promotion by anywhere from three to five years. If our own veteran directors would not choose us to act for their heirs, how could we expect other people to do so? From here on in, I'm going to concentrate on selling our trust service to our directors. Sure, I want their trusts, but even more I want them to go out and sell us to their friends. Under the right circumstances, an offhand remark from a director in the locker room at the country club can produce more new business for us than a year of advertising and a persistent campaign of personal calls.

It does not always require a great deal of effort to convince bank directors of their responsibility in that general direction. The head of a

$200 million bank's trust department recently told of an instance when the top management of his institution took several of its board members to a session of the Assemblies for Bank Directors. One speech there bore down hard on the obligation of directors to establish trust accounts in their home institutions. Within two weeks after their return, each of those directors stopped at the trust officer's desk to discuss his private situation.

Salaries are a large fraction of trust department expense and accordingly are a tempting target when budgets come under scrutiny. This is another point on which directors need sound information. Competent trust personnel is a prime necessity in any program to develop a positive profit picture, and good people for such jobs cannot be kept on salaries less than their real worth to the bank. Directors who want the trust department to develop adequate earnings must first be convinced that they cannot skimp, that they must be willing to pay for proper talent. Convincing them and keeping them are prime responsibilities of the top trust officer.

Because our own shop cannot support a salary structure for a staff of specialists such as a big city institution takes for granted, we have developed a number of part-time and cost-splitting internal arrangements that make use of particular types of expertise which are available in other departments of the bank. Part of my regular job, for instance, is buying and selling corporate bonds for our trust estates. Another officer, this one in the banking department, handles the municipals for both the bank's own portfolio and the trust department, even though these latter involve somewhat longer maturities.

Another example: Our bank, situated in the heart of a petroleum region, has a loan officer who is a petroleum engineer. This specialist devotes half his time to the trust department's gas and oil assets. We have several such split-time deals which enable us to give trust customers top-quality service at costs we can afford.

One field of new business that we cultivate at every opportunity is the development of interdepartmental alertness to trust potentialities. For example, we repeatedly point out to the loaning officers that their interests as well as those of the trust department will benefit when they keep their eyes open for situations in which trust accounts should be involved.

An instance might be a case in which we learn that a commercial customer has applied for a six-figure loan. The bank regularly requires an up-to-the-minute financial statement that goes into the applicant's resources in precise detail, even to his income tax figures.

"Fine!" we enjoy telling the loan officer. "What shape will his affairs be in for repaying all that money if he dies before it comes due? Who will be handling his estate? His widow, maybe? Will she know how to get his assets cleared of tax liabilities so the bank will be paid off in time? Could the bank just possibly be in better shape to collect promptly if his estate were in the hands of a corporate fiduciary experienced in such matters? How about asking him a few such questions before you close the loan, and perhaps suggesting that he come talk with a trust officer if the facts indicate that he should?"

It is only fair to say that the bank's loan officers are extremely co-operative in helping us find new trust business. We consciously try to develop in all of the other departments throughout the bank the same sort of interest in and awareness of what the trust department does.

Besides the shortfall in fee income because of inadequate volume, the reasons why small trust departments so often fail to earn a profit fall into a very few categories. These include inefficient operations; inadequate, split, or no compensation for certain services rendered; cost problems arising from insufficient knowledge and related causes all the way to inequitable income and expense allocation; and, all too often, acceptance of inherently unprofitable types of trust business.

Given the determination to learn, it is relatively simple to keep abreast of the most modern operational techniques. We make a point of regularly attending such meetings as the A.B.A. Trust Conferences and reading the current literature as it is published. Also, we have a competent officer in charge of trust operations, and it is his responsibility to get the necessary work performed at a low cost per unit.

Experience shows that if our fees are in any respect inadequate, no one but ourselves can properly be blamed. One point at which a trust department often encounters fee resistance is from the customer himself. We have found one simple method which obviates most customer objections. Instead of quoting him, say, a $2,400 annual fee and billing him for this amount once a year, we make it a practice to quote it as $200 a month and collect it monthly. This technique is admittedly an exercise in pure semantics—but it works. Using it has so smoothed the pathway that we are changing over most of our accounts to monthly charges just as fast as we can.

Also, we stand firm when pressure comes from either inside or outside the bank to accept a trust from a good customer—even from a director—at a rate below our regular schedule. If, for example, the banking department urges such a concession "for the good of the bank" (the most usual excuse), we will probably make a countersuggestion that the banking department obligate itself to pay the trust department the difference between our regular schedule and the amount suggested as an acceptable fee. To date no one has taken us up on this eminently fair offer.

Likewise, we invariably refuse to split fees with a cofiduciary. In fact, we explain to the prospective donor, who has come up with what obviously strikes him as an ingenious way to cut his trust costs in half, that we shall have to charge him a somewhat higher fee if the agreement provides for a cofiduciary. We point out that experience has shown us that all such arrangements use up more of our time and effort than if we were the sole fiduciary, and therefore we cannot afford to handle them at as low a fee. This ploy is amazingly effective.

A complaint commonly made by trust officers to explain unprofitable operations is that others in the bank—often pointing a finger at the banking department—call upon them to perform assorted time-consuming operations for which no compensation is proffered. Accepting some such thankless jobs is doubtless unavoidable in the interests of interdepartmental relations, but they must be kept at a minimum.

Still another money-loser generally listed is the acceptance of trust tasks of types for which a small department is unequipped. Examples are corporate trusts, H.R. 10 personal retirement trusts, and Veteran's Guardianships. There are many other types which any experienced trust officer can recite, generally from his own life story. We have our share of such costly units, but most of them are the result of errors of judgment. Our department has now been going long enough so that we pretty well know what we cannot hope to handle at a profit, and we act accordingly.

It is frequently asserted that most trust departments which lose money do so in large measure because they do not know enough about their costs. It is a fair assumption that only a few large and exceptionally well-staffed city banks have a definite and provable knowledge of their unit costs. For most of us, the expense of determining costs to three decimal places would exceed any probable benefit from the knowledge acquired. But various yardsticks are available, and failure to make use of these makes ignorance a weak excuse. Several Federal

Reserve banks, for instance, conduct periodic surveys within their own districts and are generous about passing along the resultant information. Excellent handbooks exist, such as those prepared by the A.B.A., with practical ideas for keeping trust costs under control.

Remedial action to reduce costs follows naturally, once the weak spots are revealed to management. If management will not try to determine the hard facts of costs and correct them, perhaps that bank would be better off without a trust department.

Experience and observation have convinced us that the great majority of small trust departments can be made profitable by realistic analysis of their problems and opportunities. We firmly believe that a trust department can and should be required to earn a profit after its first few lean years while it is busy accumulating a viable volume.

A trust department which after many years is still losing money probably cannot be justified for any other reason. Perhaps management should first try to encourage better performance and then have as its basic rule: Make money or else.